The Amazing Collection

Other Letters
and Revelation
Teaching Curriculum

Hebrews Through Revelation

ISBN-13: 978-1-932199-68-0
ISBN-10: 1-932199-68-3

By Big Dream Ministries

Cover design by Melissa Swanson

Some of the anecdotal illustrations in this book are true to life and are included with the permission of the persons involved. All other illustrations are composites of real situations, and any resemblance to people living or dead is coincidental.

Unless otherwise identified, all Scripture quotations in this publication are taken from the *New American Standard Bible (NASB)*.
© The Lockman Foundation 1960, 1962, 1968, 1971, 1972, 1973, 1975, 1977, 1995

Printed in the United States

INTRODUCTION TO OTHER LETTERS AND REVELATION
Set Eleven: Hebrews through Revelation

Just like the last thirteen books you have studied, the final nine books of the New Testament are also epistolary in form, written to instruct their readers in spiritual matters. The previous thirteen letters are called Pauline Epistles because the apostle Paul wrote all of them. Because these final nine epistles were written by various men, they have been labeled, for practicality's sake, the General Epistles. Their authors are James, Peter, John, Jude, and the writer of the book of Hebrews.

These letters were written over a period of approximately fifty years. The book of James was the earliest, penned between A.D. 46 and 49. Revelation was the last to be recorded; it was written by the apostle John in A.D. 95 or 96. Most of these letters were written after the Apostle Paul's death, and they carried on the Christian epistolary tradition.

In contrast to many of Paul's writings, the General Epistles were written during the years of heavy Roman persecution of the Christian population. The content of some of these letters reflects this increasingly hostile environment. In addition, the spread and strength of false teachings was much greater than during the years that Paul wrote. This challenge to Christianity is also very evident in the content and tone of these last nine books of the New Testament.

Of course, there could be no better capstone to the New Testament—and, in fact, to the entire Bible—than the book of Revelation. In it, God records His last words about the final days and the ultimate victory of His Son, the Lamb of God, and the Lion of Judah.

THE TEACHING GUIDE BULLETS/BOXES

Below is a reference guide explaining the bullet points. Do not let these become a stumbling block—they were designed to make the teaching outline easier to follow. Please note that the material presented in the boxes for "Teaching Tip," "Note," and "Application" may be used as time allows or you feel appropriate for your particular class.

Remember: your main goal is to share God's story!

▪	**Teaching Outline Points**	These are the teaching notes that come directly from the lessons taught by Pat Harley, Eleanor Lewis, Margie Ruether, and Linda Sweeney. They follow the student workbook's outline.
~	**Additional Teaching Notes**	
⋆	**Further Detail**	These are additional teaching notes that bring greater detail to each lesson.
★	**Teaching Tip**	The information contained in these boxes is designed to give you more information — whether on background or culture or context.
◆	**Note**	
❋	**Illustration**	These "stories" are designed to directly support the points being made in the lesson. If you would prefer to use personal illustrations and/or applications, please be very sure that your personal story directly supports the lesson being taught in the workbook. Don't, however, fall prey to simply sharing a good story! Text may also emphasize a point by presenting a thought-provoking question.
❖	**Application**	
✝	**Scripture References**	These are specific Scriptures being cited. We have used the New American Standard Bible (NASB).
⇨	**Summary Points**	These summarize an important "take-away" from the section being taught.
⌑	**Reviewing What We've Learned and Final Thoughts**	Repetition is a great teaching tool. These bullet points reiterate important topics with the goal to help those in your Bible study to "remember to remember." They will be used within the lesson and at the end in "Final Thoughts."

HEBREWS

Christ's Superiority

Let us also lay aside every encumbrance ...

fixing our eyes on Jesus, the author and perfecter of faith.

Hebrews 12:1–2

SESSION FIFTY-EIGHT: HEBREWS
Christ's Superiority

✝ **Memory verse:** *"Let us also lay aside every encumbrance ... fixing our eyes on Jesus, the author and perfecter of faith." (Hebrews 12:1–2)*

Introduction: The book of Hebrews introduces us to the last major section of the New Testament. Other letters and Revelation were not written by Paul as the previous thirteen books were, (though there is some discussion about Hebrews). Seven of these nine books were named after the author but the book of Hebrews was named after the recipients. Hebrews focuses on the superiority of Jesus Christ, who is superior to the prophets, the angels, Moses, Joshua, the priests, the Old Covenant, and the sacrifices. His death on the cross is the only sacrifice acceptable to God. And faith in the work of Christ is the only way to so great a salvation.

- **Oral Review:** Please refer to the **REVIEW Section** in the following Teaching Guide Outline.

- **Homework:** Because this is the beginning of a new set, homework review may not be appropriate if time has passed since completion of the last set and students do not have their workbooks with them. If they do, however, then the following questions are good for review from the book of Philemon workbook.

  Top two questions on page 104
  All of page 107
  Second and third question on page 111
  Top two questions on page 113

- **Review Helps:** Because this is the beginning of a new set, there is no written review provided at the end of the teacher presentation. If time allows, possible questions could be asked:

  What book that we have previously studied has spoken to you the most and why?
  What specific things have you learned that you did not know before you began this study?
  What has helped most in remembering the themes of the books we have studied?
  What have you learned about God?

- **Teacher Presentation on the Book of Hebrews**

- **Learning for Life:** You may choose to discuss all or just one or two of the questions on page 32.

- **Closing prayer:** Pray that your students' faith may grow deeper and wider as they begin to clearly see the vast superiority of Jesus Christ and that, by obeying Him, they will also see the vast superiority of the Christian's walk with Him.

HEBREWS
Theme: Christ's Superiority

OUTLINE AID FOR TEACHERS:

I. **THE SUPERIORITY OF THE PERSON OF CHRIST (HEBREWS 1:1–4:13)**

A. Christ is superior to the PROPHETS.

- **Hebrews 1:1–3**

    1. CHRIST created the prophets.

    2. Christ is the exact representation of the NATURE of God.

    3. He sat down at the RIGHT hand of God.

B. Christ is superior to the ANGELS.

- **Hebrews 1:4–14**

    1. He is the SON of God.

    2. The angels WORSHIP Him.

    3. The angels SERVE Him.

⇨ **WARNING #1: Pay attention to that which you have heard and do not drift away from it (Hebrews 2:1).**

C. Christ is superior to MOSES.

- **Hebrews 3:2–6**

    1. Moses was a SERVANT in God's house.

    2. Christ is the SON over God's house.

D. Christ is superior to JOSHUA.

- **Hebrews 4:8–11**

    1. Joshua could not lead the people to REST.

    2. Christ led them to His REST.

⇨ **WARNING #2: Do not harden your heart and fail to enter His rest (Hebrews 3:7–13).**

II. **THE SUPERIORITY OF THE WORK OF CHRIST (HEBREWS 4:14–10:18)**

A. Christ's work is superior to the PRIESTS.

HEBREWS
Theme: Christ's Superiority

- **Hebrews 4:14–5:10**

    1. He was tempted in all things and yet did not <u>SIN</u>.

- **Hebrews 7:23–24**

    2. Christ is superior to <u>AARON</u>.

- **Hebrews 7:25**

    3. Christ's work offers us eternal <u>SALVATION</u>.

⇨ **WARNING #3: Do not become dull of hearing (complacent, lazy, sluggish) and remain a spiritual baby (Hebrews 5:11–14).**

    B. Christ's work is superior to the Old <u>COVENANT</u>.

- **Hebrews 8:6–13; 9:11–14**

    1. He is the Mediator of a better <u>COVENANT</u>.

        a. It is written on our <u>HEARTS</u> instead of on tablets of stone.

        b. Christ's own <u>BLOOD</u> is the basis of the covenant.

    C. Christ's work is superior to the <u>SACRIFICE</u>.

- **Hebrews 9:15–10:18**

    1. Christ's sacrifice was <u>ONCE</u> and for all.

    2. He was the spotless, <u>UNDEFILED</u> sacrifice.

    3. His blood can <u>CLEANSE</u> you from sin.

⇨ **WARNING #4: Do not go on willfully sinning after receiving the knowledge of the truth (Hebrews 10:26–29).**

III.   **THE SUPERIORITY OF THE WALK OF THE CHRIST-FOLLOWER (HEBREWS 10:19–13:25)**

    A. The Christ-walk is superior in <u>FAITH</u>.

        1. The <u>DEFINITION</u> of faith is in Hebrews 11:1.

        2. The <u>EXAMPLES</u> of faith are in Hebrews 11:2–40.

    B. The Christ-walk is superior in <u>ENDURANCE</u>.

- **Hebrews 12:1–2**

        1. Christ <u>ENCOURAGES</u> us to endure.

- **Hebrews 12:5–11**

        2. The Lord <u>DISCIPLINES</u> those He loves.

- **Hebrews 12:22–24**

        3. <u>MOTIVATION</u> to endure comes from:

            a. Mount Zion and the heavenly Jerusalem

            b. The general assembly in heaven

            c. God, the Judge of all

            d. Jesus, the Mediator of the New Covenant

    C. The Christ-walk is superior in <u>LOVE</u>.

- **Hebrews 13:1–5**

        1. Love the <u>BRETHREN</u>.

        2. Show <u>HOSPITALITY</u> to strangers.

        3. Let the marriage bed be <u>UNDEFILED</u>.

        4. Give gratitude and <u>THANKSGIVING</u> to God.

        5. Be <u>CONTENT</u> with what you have.

⇨ **WARNING #5: Do not refuse Him who is speaking (Hebrews 12:25).**

Hebrews
[Christ's Superiority]

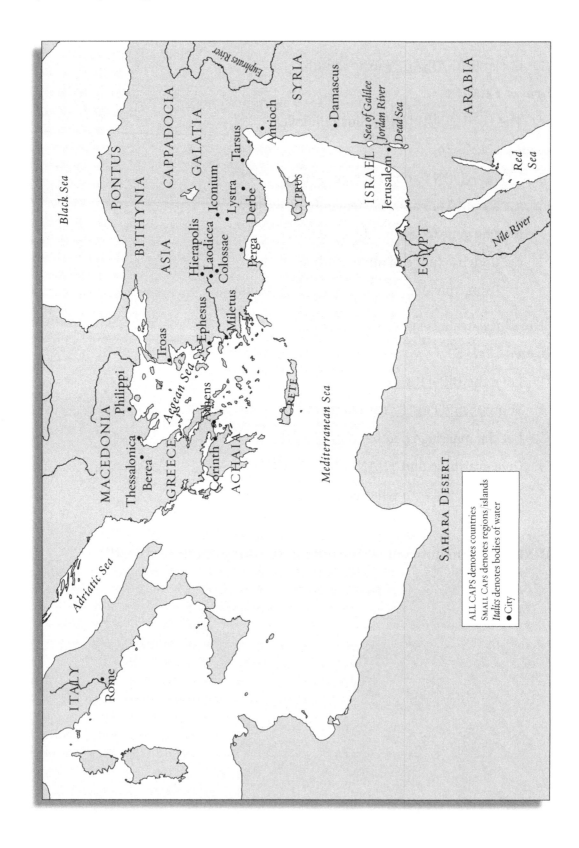

HEBREWS
Theme: Christ's Superiority

THE BASICS:
⇨ **Who: The Author:** Unknown
⇨ **What:** The superiority of Christ and Christianity
⇨ **When:** Written A.D. 64–68
⇨ **Where:** Likely recipients were the Christians living in Rome
⇨ **Why:** Exhorts Jewish Christians who were turning back to Judaism because of persecution to persevere in the faith

MEMORY VERSE: *"Let us also lay aside every encumbrance ... fixing our eyes on Jesus, the author and perfecter of faith." Hebrews 12:1–2*

****

REVIEW:

⌘ The *Old Testament History* books addressed sin, judgment, and death (the consequences of sin), and the promised Messiah.

⌘ The *New Testament History* books addressed Jesus' first coming, His time on earth, and the birth of the church.

⌘ In *Paul's Letters to the Churches*, Paul addressed the following:
  ~ **Romans:** God's righteousness described.
  ~ **First Corinthians:** Church's problems corrected.
  ~ **Second Corinthians:** Paul's ministry defended.
  ~ **Galatians:** Believers' freedom in Christ.
  ~ **Ephesians:** Believers' holy walk.
  ~ **Philippians:** Believers' joy in Christ.
  ~ **Colossians:** Believers' completion in Christ.
  ~ **First Thessalonians:** The return of the Lord.
  ~ **Second Thessalonians:** The Day of the Lord.

⌘ In *Paul's Letters to Pastors*, Paul addressed the following:
  ~ **First Timothy:** Instructions on leadership.
  ~ **Second Timothy:** Instructions on endurance.
  ~ **Titus:** Instructions on church order.
  ~ **Philemon:** Instructions on forgiveness.

OVERVIEW:

▪ As we begin Set Eleven, we are nearing the end of our great adventure through the Bible.
▪ Eight of these last nine books were written as epistles, or letters.

HEBREWS
Theme: Christ's Superiority

- The last book, Revelation, is the only New Testament prophetical book.
- These books offer an even more detailed perspective on the Christian life than was revealed in Paul's letters.
- These books are, for the most part, quite short and take up less than ten percent of the New Testament, but they offer a deeper perception on suffering, false doctrine, and Christian character.
- Except for the book of Hebrews, the epistles are named for the authors.

Brief Overview of The Books in Set Eleven
- **Hebrews:** Named for the recipients of the letter.
  - The author is unknown, but many scholars believe that Paul may have written it.
  - The purpose of the book was to assure the Hebrew readers that Christ was superior in every way to the Jewish law and traditions.
- **James:** This may have been the first book written in the New Testament. In it, he declared loudly that "faith without works is dead."
- **First and Second Peter:** In his first letter, Peter encouraged believers to stand firm in times of great suffering. In his second letter, he identified false teachers and warned against their influence.
- **First, Second, and Third John:** The apostle John wrote these letters, the gospel of John, and the book of Revelation. In these three letters, he instructed believers on how to have fellowship with God and show hospitality and he encouraged them to shun false teachers.
- **Jude:** This letter encouraged believers to contend for the faith.
- **Revelation:** This is really the culmination of the entire Bible. In it are:
  - Seven messages vital to churches today.
  - An awesome view of heaven.
  - A great battle.
  - Evil destroyed.
  - Christ is King.
  - The saints are united with Him.
  - The new Jerusalem becomes the believers' long-awaited home.

⇨ **The story that began in Genesis does not end in Revelation, but is only the beginning! The very best beginning that will continue through eternity.**

- Except for the book of James, most of these letters were written near the end of Paul's life or even perhaps after his death.
- Persecution was on the rise and false doctrine had rapidly crept into the church.

HEBREWS
Theme: Christ's Superiority

****

❋ **ILLUSTRATION:** In 1914, an advertisement appeared in a British newspaper. The ad went something like this: "Men Wanted for Hazardous Duty. Small wages. Expect bitter cold and complete darkness. There will be constant danger and a safe return is doubtful. However, if successful, there will be honor and recognition." Five thousand men applied for this position! Captain Shackleton selected twenty-seven men. His goal was to reach the mainland of Antarctica.

In 1914, the captain and his men sailed from England toward Antarctica. They were one day away from the mainland when the weather turned—storms raged, the temperature dropped. The men fought ice with the hope of reaching their destination. But, even with their reinforced hull (to work as an icebreaker), they had to stop for the night. Overnight, the temperature dropped forty degrees—from twenty above zero to twenty below. The ship was encased by ice and they soon realized that they were stuck in an ice floe. They could not move.

> ★ **TEACHING TIP:**
> *Do you think these twenty-eight men began to seriously question why they had ever agreed to this "adventure?" Do you think they experienced such thoughts as, "I want to go back to England. I should never have left in the first place."? Can you relate? Have you ever thought, "I want to go back to where I was."?*

For ten months, Captain Shackleton and his men were stranded aboard their frozen transport. Circumstances once again took a dour turn when the weight of the ice began to crush the ship. The men scrambled off the ship and stood on the ice floe. They watched as their vessel—their only hope for escape—crumbled into pieces and sank into the ocean.

****

- The book of Hebrews speaks to a group of people who wanted "to go back."
- As we stated, the author is unknown; however, some believe it was Paul, others think Barnabas, and there are those who think that Priscilla wrote this book.
- It is believed that it was written between 64 and 68 A.D. because the temple was still in place.
  - ~ The sacrificial system was still in place, which would require the temple's existence.
  - ~ The temple was destroyed in 70 A.D.
- It is thought that this epistle was written to believers living in Rome, but this is not known for sure.
- We do know that the recipients knew exactly who had written the letter.

- Why was this important to know?
  - ~ The recipients were believers who had been Jews.
    - * They had heard the message of Jesus Christ and given their lives to Him.

HEBREWS
Theme: Christ's Superiority

- - - * They had seen the power of the Holy Spirit.
    - * They had enjoyed freedom in this new religion.
  - ~ BUT their newfound freedom was being stripped away because they were Christians.
  - ~ To be a Jew was acceptable by Roman standards.
  - ~ Christianity was treated differently because it claimed to have its own king:
    - * A king who had been alive, died, and then raised from the dead.
    - * To the Romans there was only "their" king—Caesar!
  - ~ The Romans began to develop a case against the Christians, which involved an increase in persecution.

> ✶ **TEACHING TIP:**
>
> *Though the persecution was worsening at this point for believers, it was not nearly as bad as what was to come—a day when Christians would be hung on stakes and burnt alive.*

- ■ The Christian Jews could see the perilous landscape that lay ahead.
  - ~ Their land was being taken away from them, as well as their houses.
  - ~ They were being mocked. The jeering was becoming more and more uncomfortable.
- ■ The visceral response of many of these Jewish believers? "I want to go back—return to my old ways." (In other words, turn from Christianity.)

> **NOTE:** Before you get too hard on these Jewish believers, first consider their mindset.
> - ◆ Jews had been Jews for generations after generations—it was all they had known.
> - ◆ Jews knew that they were the chosen people.
> - ◆ The temple had not only represented a place to worship, but also to fellowship.
> - ◆ Their life-long friends, families, and lifestyle had been wrapped around being Jewish.
>
> ⇨ **To turn from Judaism to Christianity came at a huge personal price.**
>
> - ◆ So we can better understand how easy it would have been to question one's thinking, one's decision in becoming a Christian.

- ■ The author of Hebrews wrote to exhort them: "Don't go back. You are not safe going back, though I know it may appear that you are unsafe in your current situation. You are safe in Christ!"
- ■ The author presented a concise and clear argument that explained why these recipients should want to stay with Christianity.

⇨ **The purpose of the book of Hebrews was to show that Christ and Christianity were superior—superior to Judaism.**

HEBREWS
Theme: Christ's Superiority

I. THE SUPERIORITY OF THE PERSON OF CHRIST (HEBREWS 1:1–4:13)

- The author emphasized that the person of Christ was and is superior to anything and anyone in Judaism.

A. Christ is superior to the PROPHETS.

- We have studied the seventeen prophets of the Old Testament.
    - ~ Those prophets of old were highly respected and held in very high esteem by the Jews at this time—so the author starts with them.

<u>Hebrews 1:1–3</u>

1. CHRIST created the prophets.

- All things were made through Christ, which would include the prophets.

2. Christ is the exact representation of the NATURE of God.

> ★ **TEACHING TIP:**
> *When we observe the power, wisdom, and goodness of the Son, we are also seeing the power, wisdom, and goodness of the Father. They are one in the same—exactly!*

- The word used for "exact representation" occurs nowhere else in the New Testament—we get the word "character" from it.
    - ~ The person of the Son, Jesus Christ, is the true image and character of the person of the Father.

> **NOTE:** Consider the prophet Jeremiah. He had tremendous courage and was a very godly man—BUT he was not the exact representation of God!

3. He sat down at the RIGHT hand of God.

- No prophet ever claimed that they sat at the right hand of God.
- But, first, why is Jesus Christ "sitting?"
    - ~ The temple had no chairs, thus there was no place to sit.
        - * When a priest entered the temple, he always stood to exercise his priestly duties; and, because his work was never done, he never sat.
        - * In other words, a priest never went into the temple and sat.

- When Jesus, as the Great High Priest, entered heaven, He sat because all the priestly duties had been satisfied, completed—the priests' work was done.

B. Christ is superior to the <u>ANGELS</u>.

- Angels will be discussed in greater detail in the book of Jude.
- But we need to address the tendency of people to "worship" angels—this is seen even today.
- The author of Hebrews wants us to understand that angels should never be held in higher esteem than Jesus Christ because He is superior to them. They should not be worshiped.

<u>Hebrews 1:4–14</u>

1. He is the <u>SON</u> of God.

- Jesus Christ was *not* a "ministering spirit" as the angels were described in Hebrews 1:14.
- God the Father called Jesus His Son—from His incarnation to His resurrection and ascension to His sitting at the right hand of God.

2. The angels <u>WORSHIP</u> Him.

- In the book of Revelation, we will see a picture of heaven in which all of the angels are "worshipers"—worshiping BOTH God and Christ. (Revelation 7:11)

3. The angels <u>SERVE</u> Him.

- Angels are Christ's "ministering spirits."
  - ~ They do His bidding and work on earth.
  - ~ They minister to believers who (in His amazing salvation) are heirs with Christ.

NOTE: In the book of Hebrews, there are five very strong warnings for the recipients of this letter—but they should be heeded by believers today.
- Pay close attention to these warning in leading your class—do not skip over them.
- They are to be taken very seriously, as if God Himself were speaking to each one of us personally.

⇨ **WARNING #1: Pay attention to that which you have heard and do not drift away from it (Hebrews 2:1).**

✝ **Hebrews 2:1** "For this reason we must pay much closer attention to what we have heard, so that we do not drift away from it."

★ **<u>TEACHING TIP:</u>**

Believers should never grow complacent or indifferent toward God's Word!

HEBREWS
Theme: Christ's Superiority

~ Because of Who Jesus is—His superior and exalted position—believers need to give even greater attention to His Word.

~ Remember the Word of God that was spoken to you—whether from Jesus Himself or from His apostles.

~ Remember the power of the gospel.

~ The result of not "paying attention" to God's Word is "drifting away" from it, which is perilous territory.

****

✳ **ILLUSTRATION:** Have you ever gone to the beach, climbed upon a comfortable raft, set yourself out to float, and dozed off? What happened when you awakened? You had drifted from where you started. Because, in doing nothing, you had "naturally" drifted from where you started. (Hebrews 2:1 is an important warning to mark in your Bible!)

****

> ❖ **APPLICATION:** What are some obvious pitfalls of drifting away from God's Word?
> ~ His Truth can become less important, which leads to seeming less "relevant."
> ~ Other things (such as one's business, hobbies, sports, etc.) can become all engrossing—squeezing out time to pray or read the Bible.
> ~ It becomes easier to defer opportunities to share Jesus with others.
> ~ It becomes easier to "rationalize" ("rational"-"lies") sin in our lives.
>
> ⇨ **When we cease to pay attention to God's Word, our spiritual growth is stunted and our spiritual armor will be compromised. Such simple neglect is a powerful weapon in Satan's hands!**

C. Christ is superior to <u>Moses</u>.

1. Moses was a <u>SERVANT</u> in God's house.

2. Christ is the <u>SON</u> over God's house.

<u>Hebrews 3:2-6</u>

▪ Moses was faithful, as was Christ, but their positions were completely different.

~ Jesus is the Son: the head or the manager of the house—the Lord of the household of God.

~ Moses was the "servant"—serving in Israel, God's Old Testament household.

> ★ **TEACHING TIP:**
> *The word "house" refers to "people"—God's family.*

D. Christ is superior to <u>JOSHUA</u>.

1. Joshua could not lead the people to <u>REST</u>.

2. Christ led them to His <u>REST</u>.

<u>Hebrews 4:8–11</u>
- Joshua led God's people into the Promised Land with the goal to find "rest."
  ~ Israel, however, failed to enter the promised "rest" because of their disobedience stemming from unbelief.
  ~ Any "rest" they experienced was incomplete, unfinished.

- Jesus provided a Sabbath rest—complete and finished—that ultimately gives:
  ~ A sense of satisfaction, not exhaustion (resting from "works").
  ~ A sense of completion, as God rested after creating the world.
  ~ A sense of victory—understanding this comes through obedience to God.

⇨ **WARNING #2: Do not harden your heart and fail to enter His rest. (Hebrews 3:7–13)**

✝ **Hebrews 3:12** "Take care, brethren, that there not be in any one of you an evil, unbelieving heart that falls away from the living God."
  ~ Remember: the recipients of Hebrews were being oppressed for being Christians.

❖ **APPLICATION:** Encouragement is a powerful tool in preventing fellow believers from "falling away from the living God."
  ~ Be diligent to encourage others to press on in the Lord.
  ~ Facing suffering or persecution (as the recipients of the book of Hebrews were) can set the stage for fear to give birth to the desire to avoid the potentially painful costs of standing firm for one's faith—leading to the unintended consequence of falling away from the Lord! Encourage others!

II. THE SUPERIORITY OF THE WORK OF CHRIST (HEBREWS 4:14–10:18)

A. Christ's work is superior to the <u>PRIESTS</u>.

<u>Hebrews 4:14–5:10</u>

1. He was tempted in all things and yet did not <u>SIN</u>.

✝ **Hebrews 4:15** "For we do not have a high priest who cannot sympathize with our weaknesses, but One who has been tempted in all things as we are, yet without sin."

- "All things" included the lust of the eyes, the lust of the flesh, and the pride of life.
- Jesus Christ never sinned—he never acted upon a temptation, but He fully understands the enticements that His children face.

2. Christ is superior to <u>AARON</u>.

✞ **Hebrews 7:23–24** "The former priests, on the one hand, existed in greater numbers because they were prevented by death from continuing, but Jesus, on the other hand, because He continues forever, holds His priesthood permanently."

- Aaron died, his sons died, the Levitical priests that came after them died—their work was limited by their humanness.
- Christ lives forever—saving us and making intercession on our behalf … forever.
- In effect, God set aside the priesthood founded in Aaron.
- With Jesus Christ, the new order of priesthood was established.

3. Christ's work offers us eternal <u>SALVATION</u>.

✞ **Hebrews 7:25** "Therefore He is able also to save forever those who draw near to God through Him, since He always lives to make intercession for them."

> **NOTE:** All the sacrifices that the Levitical priests made could never eradicate sin from the heart of men—as the Law could not make a man "perfect." But God initiated a divine priesthood through Jesus Christ whose sacrifice fully atoned for sin, so that a man or woman—through faith in Christ—could be cleansed, forgiven, and enter a new, eternal relationship with God.

⇨ **WARNING #3: Do not become dull of hearing (complacent, lazy, sluggish) and remain a spiritual baby (Hebrews 5:11–14).**
   - ~ The writer stated that these recipients should all be teachers at this point.
   - ~ They, by all rights, should be mature in their faith in Christ.
   - ~ That said, they should not be thinking of going back to the Jewish faith.

> ❖ **APPLICATION:** Through studying *The Amazing Collection*, will you join us in:
>   - ~ Learning God's Word in order to live it out daily?
>   - ~ Pressing on to maturity in Christ—making it a priority of your life?

B. Christ's work is superior to the Old <u>COVENANT</u>.

1. He is the Mediator of a better <u>COVENANT</u>.

HEBREWS
Theme: Christ's Superiority

<u>Hebrews 8:6–13; 9:11–14</u>

- It is a far better covenant than what the Jews received on Mount Sinai.

    a. It is written on our <u>HEARTS</u> instead of on tablets of stone.

    b. Christ's own <u>BLOOD</u> is the basis of the covenant.

C. Christ's work is superior to the <u>SACRIFICE</u>.

<u>Hebrews 9:15–10:18</u>

   1. Christ's sacrifice was <u>ONCE</u> and for all.

   2. He was the spotless, <u>UNDEFILED</u> sacrifice.

   3. His blood can <u>CLEANSE</u> you from sin.

> **NOTE:** Why is Christ's work superior?
> - If you remember, the Jews had to continually offer sacrifices.
>   - Why? Because they would continually sin—we have sin natures (often, as the Apostle Paul claimed, doing the very thing that we don't want to do).
>   - So they would return and return and return to make sacrifices for their sin, then sin again.
> - Christ, however, offered Himself as the spotless and undefiled Lamb of God.
>   - Even though the Jews were to offer spotless lambs, they never could— because, just as with men, no animal is "perfect." (They were just getting as close to it as they humanly could.)
> - Scripture tells us that "no sin is forgiven without the remission of blood"—only Christ's blood can fully cleanse us from sin so that true, lasting forgiveness can take place. The need to frantically return to "sacrifice again" no longer exists— Jesus paid it all.

⇨ **WARNING #4: Do not go on willfully sinning after receiving the knowledge of the truth (Hebrews 10:26–29).**

✠ **Hebrews 10:26** "For if we go on sinning willfully after receiving the knowledge of the truth, there no longer remains a sacrifice for sins, ..."
   - Remember this letter was written to believers, *not* unbelievers.

HEBREWS
Theme: Christ's Superiority

> **NOTE:** In his commentary on this passage in Hebrews, Warren Wiersbe stated, "[This warning] is related to the previous three exhortations. Careless Christians start to drift through neglect; then they doubt the Word; then they grow dull toward the Word; and the next step is deliberately sinning and despising their spiritual heritage."

~ Note the sin: "willful" sin—the verb tense in this passage translates to "willingly go on sinning." The author was addressing a deliberate and ongoing choice to sin.

~ He spoke to an attitude toward the Word that God calls willful rebellion—and it was a reminder that there were no sacrifices in the Old Testament for such knowingly, presumptuous sins.

> ❖ **APPLICATION:** Have you ever willfully sinned after knowing God's truth?
> ~ To be cognizant that you are disobeying God's Word is like "playing games at the foot of the cross."
> ~ It mitigates the sacrifice of Jesus Christ to carry the notion—"I can sin … all I have to do is ask for forgiveness one more time."
> ~ Once you have seen that you have sinned, stop it! Stop it and do not continue in it.
>
> ⇨ **Believers should never take lightly the sacrifice that was required of Christ for our sin.**

▪ The author explained why he was encouraging these people so strongly:

✝ **Hebrews 10:36** "For you have need of endurance, so that when you have done the will of God, you may receive what was promised."

~ He called the believers to endure!

****

❋ **ILLUSTRATION:** Let's return to the story of Captain Shackleton. They were on an ice floe; they had three lifeboats and twenty-eight men. The men got into the lifeboats and paddled for seven days through freezing cold with very little to eat and no sure promise that they would reach land. They finally came to Elephant Island, but found it to be a rocky piece of land with little vegetation. It also represented the first time the feet of these men had stood on solid ground in approximately eighteen months. To these men, they had a semblance of stability, some solid rock to stand upon, and it was there they would stay—but they remained in a very unsafe situation.

Captain Shackleton stands as a great example of "pressing on"—he would not and did not give up. In the beginning, his goal had been to reach Antarctica; but his priorities changed when his ship went down. His focus became fixed on getting his men back safely to England—and for that one goal, he endured.

****

III. THE SUPERIORITY OF THE WALK OF THE CHRIST-FOLLOWER (HEBREWS 10:19–13:25)

A. The Christ-walk is superior in <u>FAITH</u>.

1. The <u>DEFINITION</u> of faith is in Hebrews 11:1.

- Having called the recipients to press on and endure, the author gave the greatest definition of "faith."

✝ **Hebrews 11:1** "Now faith is the assurance of things hoped for, the conviction of things not seen."

2. The <u>EXAMPLES</u> of faith are in Hebrews 11:2–40.

- In Hebrews 11, the author showed the readers what faith "looked like" by reminding them of men and women that they had grown up hearing about from Old Testament stories.
  - ~ Men and women who had persevered and pressed on because of their faith.

<u>**Hebrews 11:17–32**</u>
- Let's look at some of the author's examples:
  - ~ Abraham and Sarah: They pressed on even though they could not quite figure out what God was doing. But the "not knowing" did not make a difference because they knew obedience to God was the best thing to do.
  - ~ Moses, Gideon, Samson, and Rahab: They pressed on with great courage against seemingly insurmountable odds because they believed in God's promises.

<u>**Hebrews 11:34–35a**</u>
- Some of his examples went nameless, but what they endured for faith was recited:
  - ~ Some escaped from the edge of the sword.
  - ~ Some became mighty in war.
  - ~ Some put foreign armies to flight.
  - ~ Women received back their dead by resurrection.

<u>**Hebrews 11:35b–38**</u>
- Those examples sounded great but, then, without seeming to take a breath, the author gave the bad news:

~ Others were tortured, not accepting their release in order that they might obtain a better resurrection.

~ Some were mocked and scourged.

~ Some were chained and imprisoned.

~ Some were stoned.

~ Some were sawn in two.

~ Tempted.

~ Put to death with the sword.

~ Went about in sheepskins, in goatskins—destitute, afflicted, ill-treated, and wandering in deserts, mountains, caves, and holes in the ground.

> ★ **TEACHING TIP:**
> *Do not miss God's assessment of these faithful followers— "(men of whom the world was not worthy) …"*

▪ As Captain Shackleton had a single-minded focus for enduring, so did these faithful examples. They knew they were headed towards something that was grand and wonderful—and worth it all!

B. The Christ-walk is superior in ENDURANCE.

1. Christ ENCOURAGES us to endure.

✝ **Hebrews 12:1–2** "Therefore, since we have so great a cloud of witnesses surrounding us, let us also lay aside every encumbrance and the sin which so easily entangles us, and let us run with endurance the race that is set before us, fixing our eyes on Jesus, the author and perfecter of faith, who for the joy set before Him endured the cross, despising the shame, and has sat down at the right hand of the throne of God."

> ★ **TEACHING TIP:**
> *Just think—we are being "cheered on" by Paul and Timothy and Abraham and Moses … to name just a few!*

▪ The author encouraged these believers to "look back" to the examples of great faith he had just shared and to "look up and forward" to their greatest witness of all—Jesus!

****

❋ **ILLUSTRATION:** In the 1992 Barcelona Olympics, there was a British 400-meter runner, Derek Redmond, who was competing in the semi-final heat. As he neared the finish line, he heard a "pop" and collapsed on the track with a pulled hamstring. But he was determined to finish the race, so he got up and began to limp toward the finish line— clearly in incredible pain. The Olympic officials tried to stop him, but he pushed them away and pressed on. When interviewed later, he shared that he saw that the other runners had crossed the finish line, but he was determined to "finish the race" he had begun.

A man jumped out of the stands and ran toward the wounded athlete—race officials tried to stop him, but he would not be thwarted. When he got to Derek, he put his arm around him, whispered in his ear, and helped him finish his race. The man? His father.

Jesus calls us to run the race set before us. He is watching over us—ever ready and able to help and strengthen us to finish the race set before us. So, endure, fellow runner!

****

2. The Lord <u>DISCIPLINES</u> those He loves.

<u>Hebrews 12:5–11</u>
- The author referenced Proverbs 3:11–12 to make his point.
- The word "discipline" means "education or training … for correction"—it carries no negative connotation!
- When God disciplines, His motivation is love:
  ~ Wanting to shape our character to reflect His own.
  ~ Wanting us to press on to become a great hero of faith.

3. <u>MOTIVATION</u> to endure comes from:

✞ **Hebrews 12:22–24** "But you have come to Mount Zion and to the city of the living God, the heavenly Jerusalem, and to myriads of angels, to the general assembly and church of the firstborn who are enrolled in heaven, and to God, the Judge of all, and to the spirits of the righteous made perfect, and to Jesus, the mediator of a new covenant, and to the sprinkled blood, which speaks better than the blood of Abel."

    a. **Mount Zion and the heavenly Jerusalem**

    b. **The general assembly in heaven**

    c. **God, the Judge of all**

    d. **Jesus, the Mediator of the New Covenant**

⇨ **The author wanted these believers to remember "why" they should never turn back to their old lives!**

C. The Christ-walk is superior in <u>LOVE</u>.

<u>Hebrews 13:1–5</u>
    1. Love the <u>BRETHREN</u>.

- Love for God's people is a marker for a true believer in Christ.
  - ~ Believers will be hated by the world.
  - ~ Thus, the necessity for a believer to practically express and apply love toward fellow brothers and sisters in Christ.

2. Show <u>HOSPITALITY</u> to strangers.

- Being hospitable is a practical application of God's love for others.
- The author reminded the readers that they could be "entertaining an angel"—*as Abraham and Lot had.*

3. Let the marriage bed be <u>UNDEFILED</u>.

- The covenant of marriage is to be honored and never to be undervalued.
- Faithfulness to this relationship is essential.

4. Give gratitude and <u>THANKSGIVING</u> to God.

5. Be <u>CONTENT</u> with what you have.

⇨ **WARNING #5: Do not refuse Him who is speaking (Hebrews 12:25).**

✞ **Hebrews 12:25a** "See to it that you do not refuse Him who is speaking."

- ~ Who is speaking? Jesus! Do not refuse Jesus!
- ~ What has Jesus said through the "warnings?"
  - ⋆ Do not drift away from the Christian faith.
  - ⋆ Do not harden your heart.
  - ⋆ Do not become dull of hearing.
  - ⋆ Do not be lazy.
  - ⋆ Press on—to know Christ through His Word.
  - ⋆ Press on—to know God's ways and how to obey them.
  - ⋆ Do not go on willfully sinning—if God has convicted you of sin, be cleansed by His blood, put it behind you, and stop doing it!

⇨ **Do not refuse Jesus Christ who is speaking to you today. Endure!**

****

❊ **ILLUSTRATION:** Let's return one last time to Captain Shackleton. After spending some time on Elephant Island, he and his men came up with a plan—Captain Shackleton and two other men (brave men) boarded a twenty-two foot boat and rowed for seventeen days through some of the most hazardous waters in the entire world. Freezing cold, very little food, completely exhausted, they kept on going.

They persevered and, after about seventeen days, they reached Georgia Island upon which there was a whaling station. Good news? Yes, but there was one problem—the station was on the other side of the island! Knowing they could not get to the other side by water, after a very brief rest, the men headed out on foot. (It is important to note that this island had never been crossed before!) These determined men were not mountain climbers, but they climbed treacherous mountains, pressing on with very little sleep. For thirty-six hours they pressed on, though exhausted and hungry—finally they arrived at the whaling station. Captain Shackleton and his two men stated that they felt as if a fourth person had been with them—encouraging them, helping them to get to safety.

They were able to secure a ship and sail back to Elephant Island. Even though many weeks had passed, his men had not become discouraged because they knew their captain would rescue them and get them back to England. And he did!

However, their return to England was anticlimactic—in fact, it was hardly noticed. England was at war, so this band of courageous men returned without a lot of fanfare, honor, or recognition. The story is not complete without sharing the name of Captain Shackleton's ship that became encased in the ice of Antarctica: *Endurance*.

****

FINAL THOUGHTS AND APPLICATION

¤ Jesus Christ encourages each one of us to:
  ~ Press on and endure.
  ~ Don't look back—there is nothing for you if you go back.
  ~ Look forward—everything lies ahead.
¤ Captain Shackleton endured and completed his journey—receiving no honor or recognition.
¤ But for believers who endure to the end, they will come into the presence of Jesus and hear, "Well done, good and faithful servant."

¤ In Hebrews, the author is clear about the believer's future:
✝ **Hebrews 12:22–23** "But you have come to Mount Zion and to the city of the living God, the heavenly Jerusalem, and to myriads of angels, to the general assembly and church of the firstborn who are enrolled in heaven, and to God, the Judge of all, and to the spirits of the righteous made perfect …"

⇨ **Fix your eyes on Jesus because He is the light in heaven's glorious city. Press on toward it—endure!**

❖ **FINAL APPLICATION: Christ is better, superior, and perfect in every way.**

JAMES

Live Faith Through Works

Faith without works is dead.

James 2:26

SESSION FIFTY-NINE: JAMES
Live Faith Through Works

✝ **Memory verse:** *"Faith without works is dead." (James 2:26)*

Introduction: James was the half-brother of Jesus and, in his book, clearly explains that those who have faith in Jesus will choose to do good works because of their love and devotion for Him. This book is a practical, down-to-earth book that directs conduct for the here and now. He deals with many subjects and challenges the reader to be "doers of the Word."

- **Oral Review:** Please refer to the **REVIEW Section** in the following Teaching Guide Outline.

- **Homework:** Review the homework from the book of Hebrews.
    From pages 34–35: summarize who were the recipients of the letter and their circumstances
    Question on the bottom of page 40
    Question at the top of page 41
    Questions in pages 45–47

- **Review Helps:** Written review is provided at the end of the teacher presentation. (Optional and time permitting.)

- **Teacher Presentation on the Book of James**

- **Learning for Life:** You may choose to discuss all or just one or two of the questions on page 55.

- **Closing prayer:** Pray that those students who are going through difficult trials will be comforted knowing that God is in control and has a purpose for those times. The Christian walk is challenging but rests on the finished work of Christ and the indwelling power of the Holy Spirit. Also pray that each student would come to see the power of the tongue for great good and for great harm and hurt—and use it for good for the glory of God.

JAMES
Theme: Live Faith Through Works

OUTLINE AID FOR TEACHERS:

I. **JAMES EQUIPPED BELIEVERS TO HANDLE INEVITABLE TESTS OF FAITH (JAMES 1:1–18)**

- **James 1:2**

    A. Tests should be handled with <u>JOY</u>.

- **James 1:3–13**

    B. Tests should produce <u>BLESSINGS</u>:

    1. Endurance

    2. Maturity

    3. Wisdom

    4. Reward

- **James 1:13–16**

    C. Tests come from different <u>SOURCES</u>.

II. **JAMES EXPLAINED THE TRAITS OF FAITH (JAMES 1:19–5:6)**

- **James 1:19**

    A. Faith <u>LISTENS</u> more than talks.

- **James 1:22–25**

    B. Faith does more than listen; it <u>OBEYS</u>.

    C. Faith <u>REMEMBERS</u> what it hears and does what should be done.

- **James 2:14–26**

    D. Faith without <u>EVIDENCE</u> is dead and useless.

- **James 3:1–12**

    E. Faith <u>CONTROLS</u> its tongue.

- **James 4:1–4**

    F. Faith demonstrates godly wisdom and avoids the <u>WAYS</u> of the world.

- **James 4:7–17**

    G. Faith applies God's <u>REMEDY</u> for worldliness.

III. JAMES EXCLAIMED TRIUMPHS OF FAITH (JAMES 5:7–20)

- **James 5:7–11**

    A. Faith patiently awaits the Lord's imminent <u>RETURN</u>.

- **James 5:12**

    B. Faith will not make unnecessary, flippant <u>OATHS</u>.

- **James 5:13–16**

    C. Faith will <u>PRAY</u> during suffering *and* celebration.

JAMES

[Live Faith Through Works]

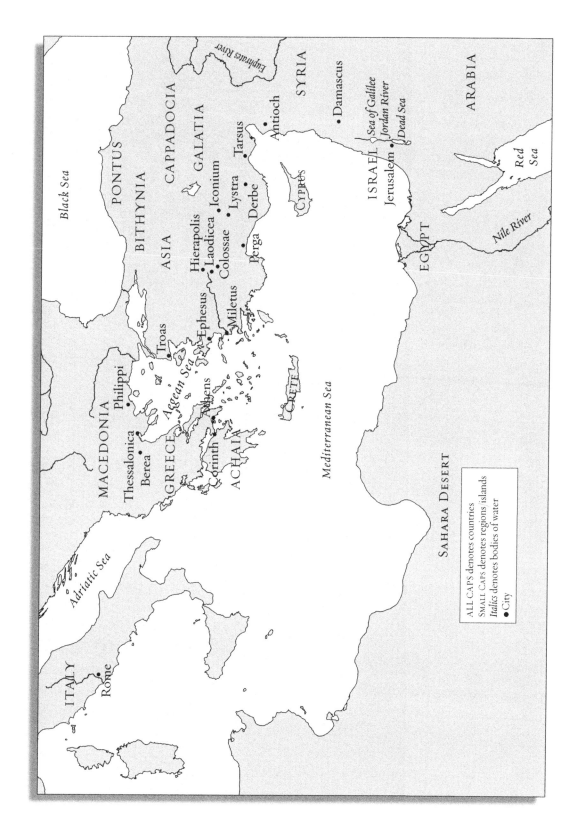

JAMES
Theme: Live Faith Through Works

THE BASICS:

⇨ **Who: The Author:** James, half-brother of Jesus

⇨ **What:** Practical book regarding Christian lifestyle under trials

⇨ **When:** Written A.D. 46–49, the earliest New Testament book

⇨ **Where:** Written from Jerusalem to Jews scattered around the world

⇨ **Why:** To instruct Jewish believers that true faith will be evidenced by works

MEMORY VERSE: *"Faith without works is dead." James 2:26*

****

REVIEW:

⌑ The *Old Testament History* books addressed sin, judgment, and death (the consequences of sin), and the promised Messiah.

⌑ The *New Testament History* books addressed Jesus' first coming, His time on earth, and the birth of the church.

⌑ In *Paul's Letters to the Churches*, Paul addressed the following:
  ~ **Romans:** God's righteousness described.
  ~ **First Corinthians:** Church's problems corrected.
  ~ **Second Corinthians:** Paul's ministry defended.
  ~ **Galatians:** Believers' freedom in Christ.
  ~ **Ephesians:** Believers' holy walk.
  ~ **Philippians:** Believers' joy in Christ.
  ~ **Colossians:** Believers' completion in Christ.
  ~ **First Thessalonians:** The return of the Lord.
  ~ **Second Thessalonians:** The Day of the Lord.

⌑ In *Paul's Letters to Pastors*, Paul addressed the following:
  ~ **1 Timothy:** Instructions on leadership.
  ~ **2 Timothy:** Instructions on endurance.
  ~ **Titus:** Instructions on church order.
  ~ **Philemon:** Instructions on forgiveness.

⌑ In *Other Letters and Revelation*, the authors addressed:
  ~ **Hebrews:** The superiority of Jesus Christ. The author encouraged the Jewish believers who were suffering for their faith to endure—not to turn back to Judaism. Nothing could compare to what they had in Christ.

JAMES
Theme: Live Faith Through Works

OVERVIEW:

****

❋ **ILLUSTRATION:** Did you learn how to behave from your parents? Did your mother or father ever ask you, "What will people think?" Usually, this was a question that was posed *after* you had misbehaved! Why would a child's behavior be important to a parent? Because a child's behavior can ultimately reflect their parents' behavior, priorities, and character.

In the same sense, James challenged the Jewish believers who received this letter to consider, "What will people think? You belong to Jesus Christ—are you acting like it?"

****

- James, the half-brother of Lord Jesus Christ, is the author of this letter.
- He became the recognized leader of the Jerusalem church in its early formation.
- Even though it is placed toward the end of the New Testament, the book of James was written between 45 A.D. and 50 A.D., making it the earliest New Testament book written.
- The recipients of this letter were Jewish believers who were scattered abroad.
  - ~ It is believed that they fled to countries across the Mediterranean due to persecution as a result of Herod Agrippa's terrible reaction to Christianity. (Acts 12)
- When we studied 2 Timothy, we discussed how it was the Christian's "combat manual"— the book of James is the Christian's "conduct manual."
- As a "conduct manual," James wanted these believers to understand and apply that:
  - ~ If they belonged to Christ, then they were to act as though they believed they belonged to Him.
  - ~ Their belief should be demonstrated or evidenced by their actions, their lifestyle.

⇨ **The purpose of the book of James was to explain that there must be evidence of one's faith in Christ.**

I. JAMES EQUIPPED BELIEVERS TO HANDLE INEVITABLE TESTS OF FAITH (JAMES 1:1–18)

- James began with a greeting in which he referred to himself as a "bond-servant" of God and the Lord Jesus Christ.
  - ~ He could have said, "I'm James ... you remember ... Jesus was my brother."

> ★ **TEACHING TIP:**
> *A bond-servant was one who was in servitude by choice.*

~ But he did not—instead James recognized his position in relation to Jesus. He was His bond-servant.

- His readers were from the twelve tribes who were scattered about in different Jewish communities because of being under great trials and pressure for their faith in Jesus Christ.

A. Tests should be handled with JOY.

✞ **James 1:2** "Consider it all joy, my brethren, when you encounter various trials ..."

- Note that James uses the word "when" regarding trials, not "if." Trials in life are inevitable.
- James' point: faith is always tested.
- Testing is designed (by God) with the purpose of bringing out the best in us.

> ★ **TEACHING TIP:**
> *God allows testing to bring out the best in us, whereas Satan wants to bring out the worst in us!*

****

❋ **ILLUSTRATION:** When airlines test a pilot to determine his ability to fly a particular type of plane, the pilot is set before a simulator that presents every possible type of scenario, including anything that could possibly go wrong while that plane is in the air. In order to fly that airplane, the pilot must past the test. If he doesn't pass the test, the pilot does not fly that airplane. (This should give passengers a sense of comfort!)

This testing is for their (and our) good. Testing has a purpose.

****

- It is important to note that there is a huge difference between joy and happiness.
  - ~ Happiness is focused on one's circumstances.
  - ~ But circumstances can change in a heartbeat—perhaps a medical exam reveals a physical problem or a phone call informs of bad news.
  - ~ Happiness can be taken away by a change in circumstances.
- James discussed "joy" because it is produced within us by the Lord Jesus Christ—it is not based on one's external circumstances.
- Joy involves the "knowing" that Jesus is:
  - ~ with us.
  - ~ taking care of us.
  - ~ in control, even in an unpleasant situation.

JAMES
Theme: Live Faith Through Works

⇨ **A believer's attitude is to be one of joy, even when going through a hard testing time.**

B. Tests should produce <u>BLESSINGS</u>:

<u>James 1:3–13</u>

1. Endurance

<u>James 1:3</u>
- The word "endurance" can be translated as "patience" in James 1:3.
  - ~ In other words, endurance is an unwavering, persevering patience.
  - ~ A good cross-reference is Romans 5:3.

2. Maturity

<u>James 1:4</u>
- Maturity is the result of endurance, developed through trials.
- Consider Joseph or Peter or Paul:
  - ~ Each of these men went through trials (testing) that helped establish their character, which enabled them to lead others.
  - ~ This was only possible because of what they had learned through enduring difficulties in life.

> ★ **TEACHING TIP:**
>
> *Remember Solomon's request of God as he became the next ruler: it was for wisdom!*

3. Wisdom

<u>James 1:5–8</u>
- Without a doubt, we need wisdom as we go through trials—so we need to pray, asking God for wisdom in a difficult situation.
- James warned these believers that they were not to be "double-minded."
  - ~ "Double-minded" suggests a hesitation, a doubting—it literally means "two-souled."
- James understood that a believer could not find stability in a trial if emotions, thoughts, and decisions vacillated—one minute trusting God and the next doubting Him.
- When we lack wisdom, God wants us to ask Him for it, believing we will receive it.

> ★ **TEACHING TIP:**
>
> *Isn't it interesting that when we doubt God's ability to answer a prayer, we experience "motion sickness" (with our thoughts tossing to and fro)? This motion sickness eventually leads us into a state of immobility—we become "stuck," unable to move ahead.*

~ If a person wonders (doubts or questions) if he will receive God's wisdom, then such unbelief will inevitably produce "double-mindedness."

⇨ **Double-mindedness reveals a lack of trust in which the communication is, "God, I do not believe You are able to or will provide the wisdom I need."**

4. Reward

- James explained that there was a progression that ultimately led to a reward:
  Endurance >> Maturity >> Wisdom >> REWARD
- The reward he speaks of is the "crown of life."

✝ **James 1:12** "Blessed is a man who perseveres under trial; for once he has been approved, he will receive the crown of life which the Lord has promised to those who love Him."

> ★ **TEACHING TIP:**
> *"We only bear the cross for a while, but we shall wear the crown to eternity."*
> *~ Matthew Henry*

C. Tests come from different <u>SOURCES</u>.

<u>James 1:13–16</u>

- As we study this letter, it is very important to recognize that there is a big difference between temptation and tempting.
  - ~ **Testing:** This word is interchangeable with the word "trial."
  - ~ **Temptation:** God does not tempt people to sin. He does not entice people into evil.
    - ⋆ Temptation comes from "self"—our old self or nature—and from Satan.

> **NOTE:** It is important to understand that trials in our lives may be both tests from God or temptations from Satan. In other words, tests can become temptations.
> - ◆ When we experience tests in our lives, God wants to use them to draw us closer to Him and to teach us a spiritual lesson.
> - ◆ The problem comes when we try to avoid or escape walking through tests or trials that God has permitted to touch our lives—we become vulnerable to temptations. What might we be tempted to do?
>   - ~ Lie (tell a falsehood)
>   - ~ Become angry, accusatory, or unkind
>   - ~ Depend on one's natural abilities versus reliance on God, aka PRIDE
>
> ⇨ **God will prove Himself to be faithful to all of His promises regarding us—if we will walk through the trial relying on Him.**

JAMES
Theme: Live Faith Through Works

****

❋ **ILLUSTRATION:** Abraham illustrated James' point in Genesis 12:10–20. Life for Abraham was going great. He and Sarah were following the Lord and experiencing His blessings. God had given Abraham great promises. All was well until Abraham encountered a trial—a famine. Instead of praying and seeking God … instead of watching to see how God would provide through this time … instead of asking God what to do … Abraham decided that they needed to run from the famine. They took off toward Egypt as their safe haven. Abraham lied and deceived others—ultimately causing great harm. He was a terrible witness for Almighty God. And he was forced to leave Egypt—in disgrace!

****

⇨ **Trying to escape trials that God has allowed will ultimately lead us out of God's will!**

✟ **James 1:17** "Every good thing given and every perfect gift is from above, coming down from the Father of lights, with whom there is no variation or shifting shadow."

  ~ James reminded these believers that God gives only good and perfect gifts.
  ~ God's gifts come from heaven above.
  ~ God is light—a light that does not flicker—and His goodness does not flicker.
  ~ God never, ever changes.

> ★ **TEACHING TIP:**
> *God desires only the best for His children!*

⇨ **Trials will come. Our response to them will display either faith or faithlessness.**

II. JAMES EXPLAINED THE TRAITS OF FAITH (JAMES 1:19–5:6)

A. Faith <u>LISTENS</u> more than talks.

James 1:19

- It has been said that this truth is supported by how we were created—two ears and one mouth.
  ~ This would suggest that we are to listen twice as much as we talk!
- God gave three instructions regarding communicating, especially with Him:
  1. **Be quick to hear**—*listen to His instructions.*
  2. **Be slow to speak**—*responses should be considered, never rash or hasty, before being spoken.*

> ★ **TEACHING TIP:**
> *There are those who are uncomfortable with the "sound of silence" and have a need to fill this space with words. Stop! Listen first.*

JAMES
Theme: Live Faith Through Works

⇨ **In trials, believers should not be quick to complain to God, but instead should listen to His Word regarding difficult circumstances—trusting and obeying Him in them.**

   3. **Be slow to anger**—*look for how God is working through a trial—be patient. Anger toward God or the trials He allows in one's life is virtually self-destructive.*

B. Faith does more than listen; it <u>OBEYS</u>.

C. Faith <u>REMEMBERS</u> what it hears and does what should be done.

<u>James 1:22–25</u>

- James did not want these believers to have only "head" knowledge of God's Word—they needed to *personally* apply it, to *personally* live it daily, in and through all of their circumstances.
- To illustrate this point, James used a visual—a mirror.
  ~ A physical mirror gives us a reflection of our image standing before it—an image of the "external"—what the world sees.
  ~ God's Word acts as a mirror, but it reflects the image of the "internal" you—what God sees regarding your heart, thoughts, etc.

> ★ **TEACHING TIP:**
> *How often people go to Bible study after Bible Study or listen to sermon after sermon, and apply what they hear to others they know—not to their own lives!*

⇨ **God's Word mirrors back how we are responding to His Word. It reveals areas of sin—of disobedience—in our lives.**

> ❖ **APPLICATION:** Have you ever gotten dressed for an event, looked in the mirror, saw something that you needed to change or fix, but forgot to do so? And then—someone took your picture! There, in all its glory, the "problem area" seemed even more pronounced!
> - ~ Can we approach God's Word in the same manner?
> - ~ Have you ever been reading His Word and become immediately convicted about an area of sin that He has "reflected" back to your heart?
> - ~ Did something else get your attention, so you forgot about the sin God had revealed to you?
>
> ⇨ **When God's Word, His mirror, reveals a flaw or a fault or a sin in your life, do not ignore it—take care of it!**

JAMES
Theme: Live Faith Through Works

D. Faith without <u>EVIDENCE</u> is dead and useless.

<u>James 2:14–26</u>
- Faith meets needs in practical ways.

✝ **James 2:15–17** "If a brother or sister is without clothing and in need of daily food, and one of you says to them, "Go in peace, be warmed and be filled," and yet you do not give them what is necessary for their body, what use is that? Even so faith, if it has no works, is dead, being by itself."

> ★ **TEACHING TIP:**
> *Remember the Good Samaritan story? Others saw a man in need and walked by without offering any help. A believer should always respond as the Samaritan did—with practical assistance!*

- Compassionate words need to be followed by compassionate deeds—they should go hand-in-hand.
- James followed this thought with a comparison: demons, Abraham, and Rahab.
  - ~ Demons: recognize Jesus and shudder. They know who He is, but they exhibit no faith in Him.
  - ~ Abraham: was made righteous by God when the Old Covenant was struck. But Abraham proved his faith when he was willing to sacrifice Isaac.
  - ~ Rahab: was the harlot in the city of Jericho. She had heard about God and what He was doing with the Israelites—she believed in Him. She risked her life (and her families') when she banked on His promises and hid the Jewish spies—and proved her faith.

✝ **James 2:26** "For just as the body without the spirit is dead, so also faith without works is dead."
  - ~ Our works (deeds/actions) prove that we have faith in Jesus—or the faith we claim is a dead faith.

> ★ **TEACHING TIP:**
> *"It is therefore faith alone which justifies, and yet the faith which justifies is not alone." ~ John Calvin*

⇨ **True believers publicly "practice" their faith through obedience to God's Word.**

E. Faith <u>CONTROLS</u> its tongue.

<u>James 3:1–12</u>
- Without a doubt, James understood man's tendency to sin with his tongue, his words.
- He compared the tongue's power to a horse's bit, a ship's rudder, and fire.
  - ~ The tongue has the power to "direct" a "bit and rudder."

> ★ **TEACHING TIP:**
> *Acres and acres of forests can be destroyed by one small spark of a single match—leaving what was once green, charred and blackened.*

JAMES
Theme: Live Faith Through Works

~ One misspoken word, whether a half-truth or a considered lie, can change the course of a person's life—it can be destructive.

⇨ **A horse needs a rider holding its rein and a ship needs a pilot manning its helm— our tongues need the Lord controlling them!**

~ The tongue has the power to destroy others.
* James explained that the tongue was unruly—having a restless evil and full of deadly poison.
* Gossip and angry words spoken can pierce the heart of others, destroying them.

> **NOTE:** Most of us have heard the phrase, "Loose lips sink ships." It is an American idiom meaning "beware of *unguarded* talk."
> ◆ This phrase became well-known and recited during World War II.
> ◆ Millions volunteered or were drafted for military duty; but these new citizen-soldiers had no frame of reference in conducting themselves in a manner that would prevent important information being disclosed to the enemy.
> ◆ Information could be inadvertently "leaked" through an innocent letter sent home or a casual conversation.
> ◆ Military movements, installations, facilities, routes, ports, movement of ships— all needed to be protected.
>
> ⇨ **In others words, silence meant security!**

■ James continued by explaining how a tongue can speak blessings, then follow with cursing—this should not be!

> ❖ **APPLICATION:** If we are completely honest, how many of us have been guilty of singing worship songs of praise on Sunday, then gossiped about someone on Monday?
> ~ Harmful, hurtful words have lasting effects.
>
> ⇨ **Once spoken, words cannot be "taken back."**

****

※ **ILLUSTRATION:** There was a little girl who had just completed first grade. She had traveled with her mother to her grandmother's farm—this was to be a nice visit. But something went terribly wrong when a conversation was overheard. The granddaughter heard her grandmother say, "She [the little girl] used to be such a pretty child, but now she has just gotten tall, skinny, and scrawny—she is not pretty like she once was." Those words changed the course of the little girl's life—they became the "mirror" to how she viewed herself. Once extroverted, she turned inward—"defining" her self-image through her grandmother's words. Words matter. Be aware—you may not know who is listening to your words.

****

> ❖ **APPLICATION:** Have you ever seen a beautiful woman or handsome man who immediately lost their attractiveness when they began to speak?!
> ~ Sarcasm and unkind or cruel comments simply are not "charming."
> ~ Consider how you talk about your spouse, in-laws, friends, and co-workers.
> ~ How would others describe your "word life?" Uplifting or brutalizing?

F. Faith demonstrates godly wisdom and avoids the <u>WAYS</u> of the world.

✝ **James 4:1–3** "What is the source of quarrels and conflicts among you? Is not the source your pleasures that wage war in your members? You lust and do not have; so you commit murder. You are envious and cannot obtain; so you fight and quarrel. You do not have because you do not ask. You ask and do not receive, because you ask with wrong motives, so that you may spend it on your pleasures."

- The world does not think to ask God for anything—worldly people hold tightly to their "independence."
- James cautioned his readers to check their motives when asking God for something.
  - ~ Do not ask of God with self-pleasure as the main motive—for selfish reasons alone.
  - ~ Wrong motives will prevent receiving from God.

<u>James 4:4</u>
- James warned of friendship with the world:
  - ~ It equates to "spiritual adultery"—the bride of Christ should not "love" the world.
  - ~ It demonstrates "hostility toward God."
    - * The "world" stands in opposition to God—it does not obey His laws or honor His position as Sovereign God.
    - * So to be its "friend" leads us to an antagonistic positon toward God.
  - * It leads to becoming an "enemy" of God.

> ★ **TEACHING TIP:**
> *Can you imagine God thinking of you as His "enemy?" Believers can make themselves His enemy if they become unfaithful to Him and live according to the ways of the world. This is tragic!*

JAMES
Theme: Live Faith Through Works

G. Faith applies God's <u>REMEDY</u> for worldliness.

(NOTE to Teachers: You may want to insert a brief illustration for one or two of the "remedies" below.)

<u>James 4:7–17</u>
- James listed God's "cure" for a believer to avoid worldliness:
  - **Submit to God's authority**—*actively yield to God's control in your life.*

  - **Resist the devil**—*actively oppose whatever approach Satan may use to tempt you.*
    - Use God's words against Satan's attacks and he will have to flee.

  - **Draw near to God**—*actively and continually come close to Him through prayer and meditating—do not keep Him at a distance in your life!*
    - His promise is sure: He will draw near to you.

> ★ **TEACHING TIP:**
> *God never leaves us—it is us who turn from Him! If God does not seem near, it is because you have moved away from Him— draw near!*

  - **Cleanse your hands, purify your hearts**—*actively get right and stay right with God.*
    - If you don't, you will become double-minded.
    - Don't act like the "old person" you were before Christ—you are a new creation.

  - **Be miserable and weep over your sin**—*actively acknowledge sin in your life, then put it out of your life.*
    - This sorrow is good because it leads to repentance and repentance leads us back from disobedience to obedience to God.

> ★ **TEACHING TIP:**
> *We need to let God exalt us, not the world!*

  - **Humble yourselves in the presence of the Lord**— *actively remember and recognize that He is God and you are not! You are not His equal.*
    - If we come to God with the correct posture and mindset, He will exalt us.

  - **Do not speak against one another**—*actively curb a critical, harsh tongue.*
    - We cannot, therefore must not, judge the heart or motives of another person— instead, address, in love, sinful actions.
    - There is only one judge and one law-giver—God, not man.

  - **Do not forget God when making plans**—*actively seek His will in all you do.*

JAMES
Theme: Live Faith Through Works

- James summed up his instructions:

✞ **James 4:17** "Therefore, to one who knows the right thing to do and does not do it, to him it is sin."

> ★ **TEACHING TIP:**
> *James 4:17 is a reminder of what was addressed in James 1:22–24.*

  ~ Sin does not only involve "what we do," but also "what we do not do."
  ~ Puritans described this as "sins of commission" and "sins of omission."

⇨ **James made it very clear—one's belief is proven by one's behavior.**

❖ **APPLICATION:** People are watching you! What are they reading from your life?
  ~ Would they be surprised to learn that you are a Christian?
  ~ Or would they acknowledge that you are "different" in how you live—your language, your actions, your kindness, etc.?
  ~ What a tragedy it would be if you lived your life in front of people and they never knew you were a Christian!

⇨ **There needs to be evidence in your life for others to clearly "see" that you are a believer in Jesus Christ.**

III. JAMES EXCLAIMED TRIUMPHS OF FAITH (JAMES 5:7–20)

A. Faith patiently awaits the Lord's imminent RETURN.

James 5:7–11
- These Jewish believers were suffering for their faith and James commended them for their endurance as they waited for Christ's return.
- James warned the people not to fall into grumbling and complaining against one another while waiting on the Lord—that would be a sinful response.
- He used several illustrations to make his point about waiting patiently:
  ~ **A Farmer:** he prepares the soil and plants the seed, but does not reap a crop instantaneously. He has to wait patiently for the harvest.
  ~ **The Old Testament Prophets:** many never saw their prophecies come to fruition and suffered greatly for what they prophesied—but they waited for God.
  ~ **Job:** the prime example of patient suffering that gave evidence that true faith can bear any trial. Also, Job had a "happy ending."

B. Faith will not make unnecessary, flippant OATHS.

✝ **James 5:12** "But above all, my brethren, do not swear, either by heaven or by earth or with any other oath; but your yes is to be yes, and your no, no, so that you may not fall under judgment."

- A believer's words should be honest, not requiring an additional "I promise" or "let me assure you."
- God made it simple regarding our words: "yes means yes" and "no means no."
- A Christian should always keep his word—period.
  - ~ If he or she does not, how then can they be believed in what they say?

> ★ **TEACHING TIP:**
> *You should be known for your word—what you say should be your bond. Your word is your bond.*

C. Faith will PRAY during suffering *and* celebration.

James 5:13–16
- Those who are suffering—pray.
- Those who are cheerful—praise.
- Those who are sick—call upon the elders to pray for them and to anoint them for healing.
  - ~ Many times, the oil that was used had a healing element in it.
  - ~ Oil is also a reference to the Holy Spirit.
- James told them that the prayer offered in faith would restore the one who was sick—and, if he had committed sins, they would be forgiven.

> **NOTE:** This may become a confusing passage to some of your students.
> - All sickness is not healed by prayer.
> - Some sickness is not healed this side of heaven.
> - We must be willing to put this in God's hands—He knows best, He is doing what is best for the kingdom and us.
> - We must be willing to accept His answer in this area.
> - We must understand that all prayers are not answered in the way we want them to be—God may respond with "yes," "no," or "wait"—He is in control and knows what is best for each one of us.

- James concluded:

✝ **James 5:16c** "The effective prayer of a righteous man can accomplish much."

~ He used the prophet Elijah to illustrate the power of prayer. (1 Kings 17)

* His dedication to and faith in God made Elijah a man devoted to prayer.

> ★ **TEACHING TIP:**
> *This speaks to a fervent prayer—one that is persistent and passionate.*

⇨ **Faith recognizes the value of prayer and praise. We need to be praying people.**

FINAL THOUGHTS AND APPLICATION

⌑ James gave practical advice on Christian conduct.

⌑ He made it clear that true faith works—if we truly believe in Jesus Christ, there will be visible evidence through our actions.

⌑ Faith endures trials because it believes and trusts in the Lord's promises.

⌑ Faith recognizes that if God allows a trial in our lives, He will use it for our good and His glory.

⌑ Our conduct—words and actions—matter because we represent Christ in everything we say or do.

⇨ **If we say that we belong to Christ, then we need to live like we do!**

❖ **FINAL APPLICATION:** **A working faith is an active, living faith. Without evidence, there is no proof that one truly believes.**

JAMES REVIEW HELPS

✧ **Divide the class into two groups and have one group stand on one side of the room and the other stand opposite to them. Each team will take a turn answering a question. Each team may work together to come up with the answer. The team that gets to twenty points first, wins!**

1. Who was the first murderer?

2. Who was the third child born to Adam and Eve?

3. Who were Abraham's son and daughter-in-law?

4. Why did Jacob flee from his parents' home?

5. How did the twelve tribes of Israel get their names?

6. Which one of Jacob's sons was in the line of Jesus?

7. Where was Jacob's family living at the end of Genesis and why?

8. Why were the Israelites enslaved in Egypt?

9. Name four of the ten plagues.

10. Who led the Israelites out of Egypt and who went with him to be the spokesman?

11. What does Passover commemorate?

12. Once they left Egypt, where did God take the Israelites for instruction and organization?

13. What structure did they build at Mt. Sinai for sacrifices and worship?

14. Why did they choose not to go into the Promised Land?

15. Who led the new generation into the Promised Land? How long did it take to conquer it?

16. What happened at Jericho?

17. Who were the judges? (job description, not names)

18. Who were the first, second, and third kings of Israel?

19. What king was responsible for the division of the kingdom?

20. What nation conquered and scattered Israel?

21. What nation conquered and exiled Judah?

22. Which two major prophets spoke *during* the exile?

23. Which two minor prophets spoke to Israel?

24. Which three prophets spoke *after* the exile?

25. Which two prophets spoke to Nineveh?

26. What woman returned from Moab with her mother-in-law and whom did she marry?

27. What woman saved the Jews from annihilation and who helped do it?

28. What woman served as a judge and led the Israelites into battle?

29. Who was the leader of the first group of Jews who returned to Jerusalem and rebuilt the temple?

30. Who also led a return to Jerusalem some years later and rebuilt the wall around Jerusalem?

31. How many years are there between the Old Testament and the New Testament?

32. Name the four gospels and tell who the audience was for each.

JAMES REVIEW HELPS
(Answers for Facilitators)

✧ **Divide the class into two groups and have one group stand on one side of the room and the other stand opposite to them. Each team will take a turn answering a question. Each team may work together to come up with the answer. The team that gets to twenty points first, wins!**

1. Who was the first murderer? **Cain**

2. Who was the third child born to Adam and Eve? **Seth (in the line of Jesus)**

3. Who were Abraham's son and daughter-in-law? **Isaac and Rebecca**

4. Why did Jacob flee from his parents' home? **Brother (Esau) wanted to kill him**

5. How did the twelve tribes of Israel get their names? **From Jacob's twelve sons**

6. Which one of Jacob's sons was in the line of Jesus? **Joseph**

7. Where was Jacob's family living at the end of Genesis and why?
   Egypt—brothers of Joseph brought them there during the famine

8. Why were the Israelites enslaved in Egypt?
   They had become mightier and more in number

9. Name four of the ten plagues.
   Water to blood, frogs, lice, flies, diseased livestock, boils, hail, locusts, darkness for three days, death of the firstborn

10. Who led the Israelites out of Egypt and who went with him to be the spokesman?
   Moses and Aaron

11. What does Passover commemorate? **God saving the Israelites as the angel of death passed over—saved by the blood on their doorposts**

12. Once they left Egypt, where did God take the Israelites for instruction and organization?
   Mt. Sinai

13. What structure did they build at Mt. Sinai for sacrifices and worship? **Tabernacle**

14. Why did they choose not to go into the Promised Land? **Afraid of the giants in the land**

15. Who led the new generation into the Promised Land? How long did it take to conquer it?
   Joshua; seven years and eighteen years to settle the land

16. What happened at Jericho? **God brought the walls down after the Israelites walked around it and shouted**

JAMES REVIEW HELPS
(Answers for Facilitators)

17. Who were the judges? (job description, not names) **Usually people who led the Israelites in war against their oppressors**

18. Who were the first, second, and third kings of Israel? **Saul, David, and Solomon**

19. What king was responsible for the division of the kingdom? **Rehoboam**

20. What nation conquered and scattered Israel? **Assyria**

21. What nation conquered and exiled Judah? **Babylon**

22. Which two major prophets spoke *during* the exile? **Daniel and Ezekiel**

23. Which two minor prophets spoke to Israel? **Hosea and Amos**

24. Which three prophets spoke *after* the exile? **Haggai, Zechariah, and Malachi**

25. Which two prophets spoke to Nineveh? **Jonah and Nahum**

26. What woman returned from Moab with her mother-in-law and whom did she marry? **Ruth returned with Naomi and married Boaz**

27. What woman saved the Jews from annihilation and who helped do it? **Queen Esther and her relative, Mordecai**

28. What woman served as a judge and led the Israelites into battle? **Deborah**

29. Who was the leader of the first group of Jews who returned to Jerusalem and rebuilt the temple? **Zerubabbel**

30. Who also led a return to Jerusalem some years later and rebuilt the wall around Jerusalem? **Nehemiah**

31. How many years are there between the Old Testament and the New Testament? **400 years**

32. Name the four gospels and tell who the audience was for each.
    Matthew—Jews
    Mark—Romans
    Luke—Greeks
    John—the world

FIRST PETER

Suffer Steadfastly

This is the true grace of God. Stand firm in it!

1 Peter 5:12

SESSION SIXTY: FIRST PETER
Suffering Steadfastly

✝ **Memory verse:** *"This is the true grace of God. Stand firm in it!" (1 Peter 5:12)*

Introduction: As Christianity grew, so did suffering and persecution. Slander, riots, local police action, and social ostracism made following Christ more and more difficult. Peter lifts the eyes of the sufferer toward heaven and paints a grand picture of what the believer **has** in Christ and who the believer **is** in Christ. He encouraged submission to the government and to one another in love. Suffering has a purpose yet, while suffering, keep focused on Jesus and rejoice until Christ has carried you through by grace and perfected, strengthened, and established you.

- **Oral Review:** Please refer to the **REVIEW Section** in the following Teaching Guide Outline.

- **Homework:** Review the homework from the book of James.

    Review pages 57–58 to gain a good understanding of who the author was
    Questions on page 60
    Questions on page 63
    Top two questions on page 64

- **Review Helps:** Written review is provided at the end of the teacher presentation. (Optional and time permitting.)

- **Teacher Presentation on the Book of First Peter**

- **Learning for Life:** You may choose to discuss all or just one or two of the questions on page 80.

- **Closing prayer:** Pray that, through this book, the students will see clearly that salvation provides hope for the future and strength for the trials they face today. Through Christ they are a royal priesthood, a holy nation, a people of God's own possession. Pray their families will bind together in mutual submission and love for one another and that God will bless each and every home.

FIRST PETER
Theme: Suffer Steadfastly

OUTLINE AID FOR TEACHERS:

I. **BACKGROUND OF PETER (1 PETER 1:1–2)**

   A. Peter was one of the twelve original <u>DISCIPLES</u> who followed Jesus the Christ.

   B. Peter was formerly a fisherman but became a fisher of <u>MEN</u>.

   C. Peter changed from an enthusiastic, impulsive coward to a solid, Holy Spirit-filled, courageous <u>LEADER</u> of the church.

II. **BELIEF OF CHRISTIANS (1 PETER 1:3–2:10)**

- **1 Peter 1:3–12**

   A. Peter described the threefold benefit of <u>SALVATION</u> for believers.

      1. Salvation provides hope for the <u>FUTURE</u>.

      2. Salvation provides strength for the trials in the <u>PRESENT</u>.

      3. Salvation was predicted and anticipated by the prophets in the <u>PAST</u>.

- **1 Peter 1:7**

   B. Peter defined salvation for the believers as <u>PRECIOUS</u>.

- **1 Peter 1:15–2:12**

   C. Peter instructed the believers in the process of <u>SANCTIFICATION</u> in order to:

      1. Be <u>HOLY</u>

      2. <u>LOVE</u> one another

      3. Desire the pure milk of the <u>WORD</u>

      4. Offer up <u>SPIRITUAL</u> sacrifices

      5. Abstain from fleshly <u>LUSTS</u>

- **1 Peter 2:9–10**

   D. Peter's purpose was <u>HOLINESS</u>

III. **BEHAVIOR OF CHRISTIANS (1 PETER 2:11–3:12)**

- **1 Peter 2:13–23**

   A. Peter ordered submission to the <u>GOVERNMENT</u>.

FIRST PETER
Theme: Suffer Steadfastly

- **1 Peter 3:1–4**

    B. Peter encouraged submission in <u>MARRIAGE</u> in order to:

    1. Win unbelieving husbands over without a <u>WORD</u>

    2. Reveal the unfading beauty of <u>INNER</u> self

    3. Have a gentle and quiet <u>SPIRIT</u>

- **1 Peter 3:7–10**

    C. Peter expected submission in all areas of <u>LIFE</u>

    D. Peter's purpose was <u>HARMONY</u>.

IV.   BUFFETING OF CHRISTIANS (1 PETER 3:13–5:14)

- **1 Peter 3:13–17**

    A. Peter challenged the believers' <u>CONDUCT</u> in suffering to be good.

- **1 Peter 4:1–2**

    B. Peter reminded the believers of <u>CHRIST'S</u> example of suffering.

- **1 Peter 4:7–11**

    C. Peter exhorted the believers with <u>COMMANDS</u> in suffering.

- **1 Peter 5:1–5a**

    D. Peter insisted the believers continue to <u>MINISTER</u> in suffering by:

    1. <u>SHEPHERDING</u> the flock

    2. <u>HUMBLING</u> themselves

- **1 Peter 5:6–7**

    E. Peter's purpose was <u>HUMILITY</u>

I Peter
[Suffer Steadfastly]

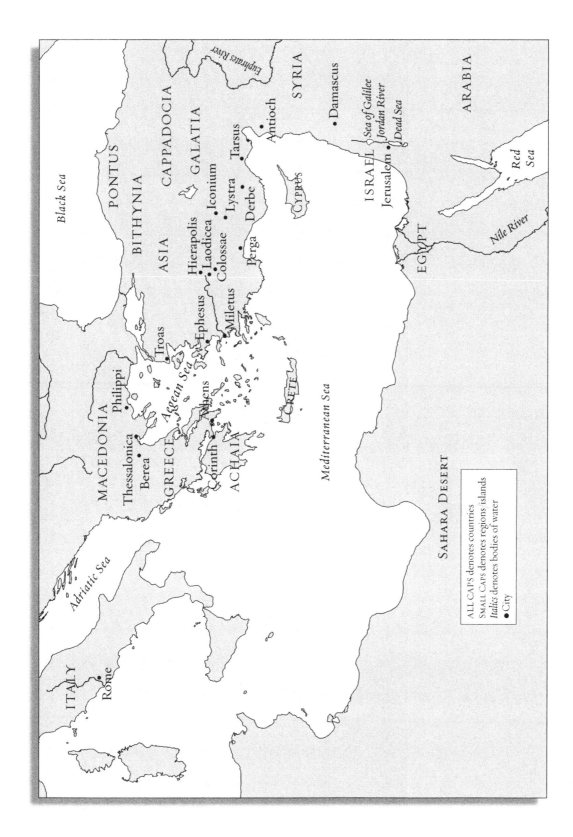

FIRST PETER
Theme: Suffer Steadfastly

THE BASICS:
⇨ **Who: The Author:** Peter
⇨ **What:** A letter written primarily, but not exclusively, to Jewish Christians under severe persecution to encourage them to stand firm in their suffering
⇨ **When:** Written A.D. 64
⇨ **Where:** Written from Rome to the churches in Asia
⇨ **Why:** To encourage the young Christians to persevere, to conduct themselves courageously, and to remain above reproach in suffering

MEMORY VERSE: *"This is the true grace of God. Stand firm in it!"* 1 Peter 5:12

****

REVIEW:
⌖ The *Old Testament History* books addressed sin, judgment, and death (the consequences of sin), and the promised Messiah.

⌖ The *New Testament History* books addressed Jesus' first coming, His time on earth, and the birth of the church.

⌖ In *Paul's Letters to the Churches*, Paul addressed the following:
  ~ **Romans:** God's righteousness described.
  ~ **First Corinthians:** Church's problems corrected.
  ~ **Second Corinthians:** Paul's ministry defended.
  ~ **Galatians:** Believers' freedom in Christ.
  ~ **Ephesians:** Believers' holy walk.
  ~ **Philippians:** Believers' joy in Christ.
  ~ **Colossians:** Believers' completion in Christ.
  ~ **First Thessalonians:** The return of the Lord.
  ~ **Second Thessalonians:** The Day of the Lord.

⌖ In *Paul's Letters to Pastors*, Paul addressed the following:
  ~ **First Timothy:** Instructions on leadership.
  ~ **Second Timothy:** Instructions on endurance.
  ~ **Titus:** Instructions on church order.
  ~ **Philemon:** Instructions on forgiveness.

⌖ In *Other Letters and Revelation*, the authors addressed:
  ~ **Hebrews:** The superiority of Jesus Christ. The author encouraged the Jewish believers who were suffering for their faith to endure—not to turn back to Judaism. Nothing could compare to what they had in Christ.

FIRST PETER
Theme: Suffer Steadfastly

~ **James:** Addressed true faith—it will have works to prove it.

OVERVIEW:

****

❋ **ILLUSTRATION:** It started out as a typical day for a seventeen year old high school student. Never did she imagine that a gun would be pointed directly at her face and she would be asked by a fellow student, "Do you believe that Jesus Christ is Lord?" But there she stood and responded, "Yes, I do." It was reported that the shooter asked, "Why?"—but never gave her a chance to respond before pulling the trigger. She was killed that day in 1999 in Littleton, Colorado—the high school was Columbine.

****

- In the book of 1 Peter, the apostle called for believers to stand firm and be ready to give an accounting for their faith, even in the face of persecution, and to not be surprised by any attack on their Christian stance—the student in our illustration answered Peter's call to steadfast faith.
- Peter wrote this book toward the end of his life.
- He stated that he wrote it from Babylon, a symbolic name used for Rome by writers who wished to avoid trouble with Roman authorities.
- He referred to the recipients of his letter as "sojourners of the dispersion."

> ★ **TEACHING TIP:**
>
> *"Sojourners of the dispersion" should be a familiar phrase, as we studied this term in the books of the exiles.*

  - ~ When the faithful Jews were exiled to Babylonia, the prophets of the Old Testament referred to them as "sojourners, travelers, or scattered ones."
- Given that backdrop, most commentators believe Peter's audience was Jewish Christians.
  - ~ Some even believe that these were new Jewish Christians who were being baptized—making their faith all the more public.
  - ~ Their alignment to Christ would put them under greater scrutiny leading to even greater persecution.
- With the flames of persecution heating up, Peter saw two things:
  1. Though the first century church had basically been divided into Jew and Gentile factions, the persecution was forming them into one, new identity in Christ.
  2. These believers were being scattered all the more, which resulted in spreading the Christian faith—the exact opposite of Rome's intent.
- The Romans did not know what to do with "Christians."
  - ~ Were they simply a part of a Jewish sect? If so, Judaism was legal.

~ Or were they their own religion? If so, Christianity was to be outlawed. Peter saw the tide of intolerance heating up against believers.

- For a Jewish Christian or a Christian, in general, the landscape of life changed dramatically:
  ~ They were harassed.
  ~ They were socially exiled.
  ~ Many times their businesses were shunned.
  ~ They were asked to leave their community.
  ~ Some were beaten, while others were driven from their homes.
  ~ At the very least, they were put out of the synagogue—cut off from their very own families.

- Peter understood their plight because he had witnessed and experienced persecution first-hand.
  ~ He had seen Jesus Christ suffer, be slandered, be rejected, be abandoned. But in all of this, Jesus had stood firm.
  ~ Peter himself would be martyred for his faith.
    * Tradition states that he himself was crucified, but he had insisted on being crucified upside down because he did not consider himself worthy to die in the same manner as his Lord.

⇨ **The purpose of the book of 1 Peter is to encourage believers to steadfastly stand firm for Jesus Christ—no matter the suffering it may bring.**

I. BACKGROUND OF PETER (1 PETER 1:1–2)

A. Peter was one of the twelve original <u>DISCIPLES</u> who followed Jesus the Christ.

- At the beginning of His public ministry, Jesus called Peter to "Follow Me!"
- At the very end of His time on earth, Jesus said to Peter, "You *must* follow Me."

> **NOTE:** One lesson that we learn from Peter's life is that it is better to follow and fail, than not follow at all.
> - He would follow and then trip.
> - He would follow and then sink.
> - He would follow and then run away.
> - BUT Peter followed until the end!

- Peter was known by several names—Cephas, Simon Peter, and "the rock."

FIRST PETER
Theme: Suffer Steadfastly

- He was part of Jesus' inner circle with James and John.
- He witnessed the transfiguration of Jesus Christ. Jesus wanted Peter to fully understand that He was the Christ, the promised Messiah.

B. Peter was formerly a fisherman but became a fisher of <u>MEN</u>.

- The very writing of this letter evidenced this fact.
- Peter's background involved a fishing business with his brother, Andrew, and his cousins, James and John of Zebedee.
- When Jesus called him, he followed Him, and never looked back.

C. Peter changed from an enthusiastic, impulsive coward to a solid, Holy Spirit-filled, courageous <u>LEADER</u> of the church.

- Peter's life demonstrates an important lesson—enthusiasm without the indwelling and filling of the Holy Spirit can be calamitous.
- Some attribute the phrase—"Never say never"—to Peter.
  - ~ Consider the number of times he uttered, "Never."
    - * I will never leave You.
    - * I will never desert You.
    - * I will never let You wash my feet.
    - * I will never let You die.
- Peter did, however, desert Christ, yet later, after he was indwelt by the Holy Spirit:
  - ~ He became known as the voice of the Pentecost.
  - ~ He boldly went before the Sanhedrin (those he ran from on the night of Christ's trial) and boldly said, "I cannot deny my Lord. I have to tell the world who He is."
    - * And he did so for the rest of his life.
  - ~ Tradition states that Peter and his wife went from place to place planting churches and confirming the faith.

⇨ **Peter became known as the "apostle of hope"—hope in suffering.**
  - ~ Only Christ Jesus can take a coward and turn him into a man with a message of hope, even in suffering.

II. BELIEF OF CHRISTIANS (1:3–2:10)

A. Peter described the threefold benefit of <u>SALVATION</u> for believers.

- Peter personally saw Christ provide salvation to others.

FIRST PETER
Theme: Suffer Steadfastly

✝ **1 Peter 1:3** "Blessed be the God and Father of our Lord Jesus Christ, who according to His great mercy has caused us to be born again to a living hope through the resurrection of Jesus Christ from the dead …"

- Salvation provides a "living hope"—Peter wanted them to remember this in their suffering.

1. Salvation provides hope for the FUTURE.

1 Peter 1:4
- This "living hope" promised a "lasting" hope—an imperishable inheritance, one that will not fade away—reserved in heaven.
- He wanted these believers' focus to be upward and forward!

2. Salvation provides strength for the trials in the PRESENT.

1 Peter 1:5–9
- They could know that the Lord was watching over them, giving them strength.
- The idea here is a "faithful guardianship" that was exercised over them by God to preserve them in their faith and hope in the gospel—in the midst of their trials.
- They should not put their faith in men, but in the Lord who would be found faithful.

> ★ **TEACHING TIP:**
> *This message is very relevant today! There are still thousands of Christians being martyred every year.*

3. Salvation was predicted and anticipated by the prophets in the PAST.

1 Peter 1:10–12
- The prophets spoke about the coming Messiah—His first and second coming—though they did not fully understand the timing or circumstances that would unfold.
- Peter had been an eyewitness to Christ's first coming and he had confident hope that Christ would come again!

B. Peter defined salvation for the believers as PRECIOUS.

- As you do your homework this week, pause and reflect upon what Peter reminded his readers as "precious:"
    - ∼ 1 Peter 1:7   One's faith is precious
    - ∼ 1 Peter 1:19   Christ's sacrificed blood is precious
    - ∼ 1 Peter 2:4,6–7   Christ, the cornerstone, is precious
    - ∼ 1 Peter 3:4   The Holy Spirit within is precious
    - ∼ 2 Peter 1:4   God's promises are precious

C. Peter instructed the believers in the process of <u>SANCTIFICATION</u> in order to:

1. Be <u>HOLY</u>

✟ **1 Peter 1:15–16** "... but like the Holy One who called you, be holy yourselves also in all your behavior; because it is written, "YOU SHALL BE HOLY, FOR I AM HOLY.""

- The word "holy" means to be set apart *to* God.
- Believers are to lead a holy lifestyle because they represent God.
- The believers to whom Peter was writing were suffering, being persecuted, but they were still called to "be holy."
  - ~ This would be possible through the enabling power of the Holy Spirit.

> ★ **TEACHING TIP:**
> *Peter was not calling these believers to "sinless perfection"—rather he was reminding them that they had been set apart to God as His children. They needed to respond like His children—even in suffering.*

⇨ **Believers profess to be people of God. Their conduct and character should seek to imitate His holiness—no matter their circumstances.**

2. <u>LOVE</u> one another

✟ **1 Peter 1:22** "Since you have in obedience to the truth purified your souls for a sincere love of the brethren, fervently love one another from the heart, ..."

- Peter called for an active, fervent love for other believers.
  - ~ He called them to have a "brotherly" love (Greek, *phileo*) by demonstrating a "divine" love (Greek, *agape*).
    - ✶ Brotherly love is based on "*because* of who you are."
    - ✶ Agape love is based on "*in spite* of who you are."
  - ~ The word "fervent" means "intently"—in other words, this is an active decision.

> ★ **TEACHING TIP:**
> *An unbeliever can demonstrate "brotherly" love. BUT "agape" love is only possible if a person is controlled by the Holy Spirit.*

> **NOTE:** Often an active love for another person and the decisive rejection of sin or evil are yoked together.
> - ◆ To live a life of "holiness" requires both—you do not have one without the other.

- Peter explained how they were to love one another:

✞ **1 Peter 2:1** "Therefore, putting aside all malice and all deceit and hypocrisy and envy and all slander, ..."

- ~ What is the "therefore" there for? It ties back to living a life of holiness and loving the brethren.
- ~ "Put aside" means to "lay aside" or "cast off" something *entirely*. That is, they were no longer to practice certain behavior.
- ~ What were they to put aside?
  - ∗ **ALL malice:** this refers to ill-will toward another with a desire to injure without cause—hurting another for personal gratification.
  - ∗ **ALL deceit:** deceit of all kinds—dishonesty, deception, pretenses, etc.
  - ∗ **ALL hypocrisy:** pretending to be what you are not—a false godliness that hides a heart with evil intentions.
  - ∗ **ALL envy:** hatred for others because of something they have—whether a character trait or a possession.
  - ∗ **ALL slander:** speaking against others—it infers "backbiting."

> ★ **TEACHING TIP:**
> *These are traits we can learn and acquire through our lifetimes— they are common mindsets of the world.*

3. Desire the pure milk of the <u>WORD</u>

<u>1 Peter 2:2–3</u>
- Peter used the illustration of newborn babies to make his point regarding the attitude a believer should have toward the Word of God:
  - ~ Babies need wholesome milk to grow and thrive. Believers need the Word of God to spiritually grow and thrive.
  - ~ As milk nourishes and refreshes a child, the Word of God does the same for the believer.

4. Offer up <u>SPIRITUAL</u> sacrifices

<u>1 Peter 2:4–10</u>
- These were Jewish believers so they knew about the requirement of sacrifices taught in the Old Testament. They knew about sacrificing animals.
- Peter wanted them to understand that God wanted their sacrifice to be the believer himself—a "sacrificed life."

> ★ **TEACHING TIP:**
> *Such a spiritual sacrifice would seem to require a heart that sought to "be holy" as God is holy.*

- Peter wanted them to understand that God desired lives that had been "transformed"—internally and spiritually.

2 Peter 2:8

- Peter used an analogy with which he was well-acquainted: rocks, stones.
- He called these believers "living stones" built upon the precious cornerstone, Jesus Christ—this is the church.
- Believers are to actively serve Him in this "living" church!

⇨ **In contrast to believers, Peter explained that unbelievers would find Christ Jesus to be a "stone of stumbling"—they will constantly and continually "trip" over Him due to their unbelief and disobedience.**

> ★ **TEACHING TIP:**
>
> *The cornerstone in building is also known as the "foundation" stone or "setting" stone. It is the first stone set in the construction of a masonry foundation—the most important because all other stones will be set in reference to this stone. It determines the position of the entire structure.*

5. Abstain from fleshly LUSTS

1 Peter 2:11–12

- Peter reminded his readers that they were "aliens" in a foreign land and, as such, were "ambassadors" for Christ wherever they journeyed.
- In their traveling, they were to live *differently*—be holy—and not succumb to living *like* the cultures they passed through as "pilgrims."

D. Peter's purpose was HOLINESS.

1 Peter 2:9–10

- Peter wanted these believers to remember that they were the people of God:
  - ~ A people for His own possession
  - ~ Called out of darkness into His marvelous light
  - ~ Recipients of His mercy
- Such a relationship in and with God separated them from the world. They had been called to be different from the world, to be a holy people.

⇨ **The constant and supreme purpose of a Christian "pilgrim" is to be holy and to represent their Holy Father.**

III. BEHAVIOR OF CHRISTIANS (1 PETER 2:11–3:12)

- Peter began his instructions on the behavior of believers with "submission."
  - ~ Submission is not a popular concept in our culture today.

~ However, in Peter's time, the idea of "submission" was part of the Roman culture.

    ✶ The Romans watched their military demonstrate it.

    ✶ To "submit" meant to be "subject to someone else, to respect their authority, to obey."

A. Peter ordered submission to the <u>GOVERNMENT</u>.

1 Peter 2:13–17

▪ He instructed them to honor the authority that was in place.

▪ He said that this was to be done for "the Lord's sake." (1 Peter 2:13)

    ~ God required this of His followers.

    ~ It was God who had entrusted power to these human institutions and leaders.

        ✶ If God put a person in a certain position, then we must demonstrate our trust of God by honoring the position of leadership.

> ✶ **TEACHING TIP:**
> *Believers may not respect the man or woman who leads, but they must respect the office of leadership and obey the laws of the land.*

> **NOTE:** No doubt, the recipients of his letter may have wanted to rebuff this instruction, rationalizing, "These leaders are harsh and unjust. They are persecuting us."
> ◆ Peter most certainly understood their circumstances, but a believer's call to submissi[on] was not based on their situation, but on obedience to God.

1 Peter 2:18–20

▪ Peter used a radical illustration to make his point—a slave serving a cruel master.

    ~ Slaves were called to be submissive to even unreasonable masters.

    ~ Their submission was not contingent on whether their master was kind or not.

▪ In the same manner, a Christian is called to submit to the authorities in control.

⇨ **Jesus Christ demonstrated submission to earthly authorities—He is our example.**

✝ **1 Peter 2:21–23** "For you have been called for this purpose, since Christ also suffered for you, leaving you an example for you to follow in His steps, WHO COMMITTED NO SIN, NOR WAS ANY DECEIT FOUND IN HIS MOUTH; and while being reviled, He did not revile in return; while suffering, He uttered no threats, but kept entrusting Himself to Him who judges righteously …"

> ✶ **TEACHING TIP:**
> *The question "What would Jesus do?" was prompted by these verses.*

B. Peter encouraged submission in <u>MARRIAGE</u> in order to:

> NOTE: This is not a popular topic, especially with women. It is important that Peter's teaching is put in context.
> - He begins with the phrase "in the same way." In what "same way?"
>   - ~ In Christ's example just set forth in the previous verses!
> - Encourage your women to focus on "following in His steps"—not following the cultures'!
> - Remind them that obedience to God is for our own good and for His glory.

- Within Peter's audience, many Christian women were married to unbelieving Roman men.
- In that day, the Roman man had complete authority over his family.
  - ~ He could have her dismissed from his home.
  - ~ He could divorce her without cause.

- Understanding that backdrop, Peter did not tell these women to evangelize passionately with words, but to submit passionately with actions. He explained why:

1. Win unbelieving husbands over without a <u>WORD</u>

<u>1 Peter 3:1–2</u>
- This is a bold statement—to win someone to Christ without a word. How could this happen?
  - ~ God is sharing the power of "living out" one's belief.
  - ~ A Christian wife's behavior should deliver a strong message regarding what she believes about Jesus— it should reflect her faith and love for the Lord.

- Most importantly, Peter explained the "why" behind this instruction to submit:
  - ~ Such action/attitude could win an unbelieving spouse to the Lord.

2. Reveal the unfading beauty of <u>INNER</u> self

<u>1 Peter 3:3</u>
- A wife's focus should be on a lasting beauty makeover—Jesus Christ living within!
  - ~ The Lord produces loveliness within a woman that supersedes any product that may be sold in a store.
  - ~ The world's definition of beauty is ever-changing and external. The inward beauty of a believing wife does not change (in fact, it grows sweeter with age) and is eternal.

- Peter was not finding fault with wives who wanted to "look good" for their husbands—rather he was presenting the priorities of beauty and it should begin inward with the Lord.
- He understood that inward beauty had a magnetic appeal because of its source.

3. Have a gentle and quiet SPIRIT

1 Peter 3:4

- The question may be asked, "But what if I have an outgoing personality? I'm gregarious! In fact, my husband loves that I'm an extrovert!"
- Peter was not addressing personality types—he was speaking to a spirit-controlled mind.
- He wanted these Christian wives to understand the invaluable witness they had by demonstrating a gentle and quiet spirit.

> ❖ **APPLICATION:** How would this look practically?
>   ~ It is a calm spirit—even tempered, not easily agitated.
>   ~ It is a contented spirit—not envious and constantly complaining.
>   ~ It is free from pride—not continuously "competing" with others, whether fashion, possessions, etc. (especially with other women).
>
> ⇨ These are not the qualities of a "weak" woman! They require a strong heart and will—consciously choosing devotion to God over "self" ("my rights").

****

❋ **ILLUSTRATION:** A young woman saw Peter's instructions lived out through her mother and it impacted her family. She was actually in college before her mother came to Christ. Immediately, well-meaning Christians told her mother, "You need to clean your house out! Get rid of all the men's magazines he likes and replace them with a Bible and different devotions. He will surely get the message!" It did not take this wife long to realize that this was a very ineffective approach to win over her husband. She decided to prayerfully live out Peter's instructions in 1 Peter 3:1–4. Without a word (or lecture!), the husband saw his wife transformed. The daughter shared, "We were like dominos! Dad was the first to follow my mom, then me, and then my brother! Her gentle and quiet spirit won over our entire family!"

The daughter asked her mom how she accomplished such obedience to this Scripture. Her mother responded, "Someone shared a quote with me. It was supposedly spoken by St. Francis of Assisi—'Preach the Gospel at all times. When necessary, use words.'"

****

FIRST PETER
Theme: Suffer Steadfastly

⇨ **Submission is all about God—are we willing to come under His authority and obey Him?**

C. Peter expected submission in all areas of <u>LIFE</u>.

> **NOTE:** If there is time and it seems appropriate to your specific class, take time to share that Peter addressed husbands as well. (1 Peter 3:7)
> - He started with an important phrase, "in the same way."
> - A husband should demonstrate a similar attitude of love and respect toward his spouse, as Peter had instructed wives.
>   - ~ His wife should hold a special place of honor in his life.
>   - ~ He should treat her with tenderness.
>   - ~ He should recognize her spiritually as his equal.
>
> ⇨ **This would have been considered radical teaching to men in this culture.**

1 Peter 3:7–10

- Peter wanted them to realize that God was sovereign and, as such, had the authority to place people in authority over others—whether government, employer, or husband.
- He basically called these Jewish believers to trust God with those who were over them.
- Peter took a "page" from Psalm 34:12–16 to make his point:
  - ~ Don't return evil for evil.
    - * Rather than "explode" in anger at someone, "explode" in love!
  - ~ Turn away from evil.
    - * To those who would persecute you, love them in return!

> ★ **TEACHING TIP:**
> *This was radical thinking, but it was straight from the Lord. His Word taught this and He lived it out—all the way to the cross.*

⇨ **Remember: Follow Jesus Christ's example—follow in His steps! (1 Peter 2:21)**

D. Peter's purpose was <u>HARMONY</u>.

✞ **1 Peter 3:8–9** "To sum up, all of you be harmonious, sympathetic, brotherly, kindhearted, and humble in spirit; not returning evil for evil or insult for insult, but giving a blessing instead; for you were called for the very purpose that you might inherit a blessing."

- Harmony defines the church—such unity will look different to the world.

IV.   BUFFETING OF CHRISTIANS (1 PETER 3:13–5:14)

- If submission was a tough topic, Peter followed with an even tougher one—suffering.
- Peter used seven different Greek words for the word "suffering." Their meanings included:
    ~ Physical pain: they would experience physical persecution.
    ~ Mental anguish: that which would weigh heavy on their minds.
    ~ Emotional pain: that which they would never expect.
    ~ A looming terror of disaster
    ~ Crucifixion: the worst way to die—the most gruesome and humiliating death.

> **NOTE:** Both Jesus and Peter suffered the horrible fate of crucifixion. In this letter, Peter seemed to have reached a deeply held conclusion: holiness is the *awareness* and the *acknowledgement* and *acceptance* that suffering is allowed by God.

- God does not allow suffering or pain in our lives to "trip" us up, but rather to test our faith and to bring Him glory.
- Peter commissioned these Jesus believers to face suffering in a certain manner.

A. Peter challenged the believers' <u>CONDUCT</u> in suffering to be good.

1 Peter 3:13–17
- It is very important to note that the suffering Peter addressed was a consequence of standing firm in their faith—NOT for sin (though the Bible definitely correlates sin and suffering, but not in this context).

- Peter encouraged them to put their suffering to good use, as a platform:
    ~ Be ready to make a defense of the "hope" that was in them—even in the midst of suffering.
    ~ Respond with gentleness and reverence—maintaining a good conscience.
    ~ Put those who persecute you to shame by exhibiting Christ-like behavior.

- No doubt, this was a hard message to receive, but Peter summed it up:

> **★ TEACHING TIP:**
> *Unbelievers may accuse us, but God knows our heart. Keep on doing what is right in His eyes!*

✝ **1 Peter 3:17** "For it is better, if God should will it so, that you suffer for doing what is right rather than for doing what is wrong."

⇨ **When you suffer for your faith in Christ Jesus, suffer well.**

FIRST PETER
Theme: Suffer Steadfastly

B. Peter reminded the believers of <u>CHRIST'S</u> example of suffering.

<u>1 Peter 4:1–2</u>
- It is important to remember what Jesus experienced while He walked this earth:
  - ~ Hunger
  - ~ Physical pain
  - ~ Loneliness
  - ~ Abandonment
  - ~ Rejection from the very people He came to save
- How did He respond to this suffering? Without sin!

- As Peter penned this letter, he very likely remembered Jesus' words, "If the world hates you, you know that it has hated Me before it hated you." (John 15:18)

> ★ **TEACHING TIP:**
> *How can we follow Jesus' example? By continually entrusting ourselves to God—just as Jesus did. (1 Peter 2:23)*

⇨ **As believers, Jesus Christ is our example on "how" to respond to suffering for one's faith.**

C. Peter exhorted the believers with <u>COMMANDS</u> in suffering.

<u>1 Peter 4:7–11</u>
- Peter called the believers to basically live their lives well, glorifying Jesus Christ, even in times of suffering or persecution for their faith.

- As such he called them to continue to:
  - ~ Pray.
  - ~ Keep fervent in their love for one another.
    - ⋆ A love that stretches far and beyond, never reaching a "breaking point."
  - ~ Be hospitable—without complaint.
    - ⋆ Open their homes—a practical response of their love for one another.
  - ~ Use your spiritual gift—serve others through it.
    - ⋆ No matter the circumstances, they were to "minister" to one another. God would provide the grace and strength to do so.

⇨ **Believers have a responsibility to one another in the midst of suffering or persecution for the faith.**

D. Peter insisted the believers continue to <u>MINISTER</u> in suffering by:

1. <u>SHEPHERDING</u> the flock

FIRST PETER
Theme: Suffer Steadfastly

1 Peter 5:1–5a

- Peter began by exhorting the elders, shepherds and overseers directly: they were to be an example to their flocks.
- He did not discount their persecution, suffering, or pain.
- Peter did, however, instruct them to continue to minister to their flocks—believers in their midst. He reminded them how they were called to minister:
  - ~ *Lead*
    - * Sheep will go their own way without a shepherd. Lead them in God's way.
  - ~ *With a willing heart*
    - * Do not view this as "just a job," but with a ministry to serve God.
  - ~ *Without a dictatorial spirit*
    - * Live out your faith through a godly life and sacrificial service—others will respect and follow you.
- Peter also reminded them that there would be a heavenly reward.
  - ~ Submit to the Chief Shepherd, Jesus Christ.
  - ~ Seek to please Him and glorify Him alone.

> **★ TEACHING TIP:**
> *This is true for believers today—stay faithful in what God has called you to do—no matter your circumstances!*

2. __HUMBLING__ themselves

- Peter followed his instructions to the spiritual leaders to the "young men" in the fellowship of believers: "... be subject to your elders." (1 Peter 5:5a)
  - ~ In other words, continue to respect and honor their authority.

> **★ TEACHING TIP:**
> *This call to humility is one to all believers because it continues Peter's call to submission—to God and to those He has put in leadership.*

E. Peter's purpose was __HUMILITY__.

✞ **1 Peter 5:6** "Therefore humble yourselves under the mighty hand of God, that He may exalt you at the proper time ..."

- This verse summed up Peter's purpose of writing this letter:
  - ~ Suffering will bring humility.
  - ~ In that humility, God will be exalted.
  - ~ Eventually, the believer will be rewarded and glorified.

✞ **1 Peter 5:7** "... casting all your anxiety on Him, because He cares for you."

- Suffering brings anxiety, apprehension, angst—the only way to combat these negative feelings is to give them over to Jesus Christ.

1 Peter
67

FIRST PETER
Theme: Suffer Steadfastly

- This is only possible when we fully trust in and rely on His love for us—His absolute, unchanging care for us.

- After writing a letter about the certainty of suffering for one's faith in Jesus Christ, Peter ended this letter with the certainty of the peace found in Christ:

✝ **1 Peter 5:14b** "Peace be to you all who are in Christ."

~ We can cast our anxious thoughts to God because His strengthening, peace-giving grace is with us no matter what happens.

FINAL THOUGHTS AND APPLICATION

- Many of you taking this study are suffering for your faith:
  ~ Perhaps your own family has ostracized you because of your faith in Jesus Christ.
  ~ Or you have or are facing circumstances that you never imagined a loving God would allow you to face.
- Trust God in times of suffering. There is a plaque that reads, "And, if not, God is still good."
  ~ God's love, strength, goodness, and grace never, ever change.
- Submit to Him in all of your circumstances—His presence and peace are close by.

- ❖ **FINAL APPLICATION:** During times of crisis, suffering, and confusion, do you show the Christ-like characteristics of holiness, harmony, and humility?

FIRST PETER REVIEW HELPS

◇ **Bible Charades:** Choose twenty Bible characters. Break into two teams. Using the idea of the game Charades, have each team take turns acting out the people. The team who guesses the names the fastest wins.

<u>Possible people for Charades:</u>

- Moses
- Joshua
- David
- Deborah
- Solomon
- John the Baptist
- Adam and Eve
- Peter
- Zacchaeus
- Lazarus

- Mary, mother of Jesus
- Abraham
- Jacob
- Joseph
- Peter
- Martha
- Dorcas
- Daniel
- Esther
- Jonah

1 PETER

SECOND PETER

Identify False Teachers

Be on your guard so that you are not carried away

by the error of unprincipled men.

2 Peter 3:17

SESSION SIXTY-ONE: SECOND PETER
Identify False Teachers

✞ **Memory verse:** *"Be on your guard so that you are not carried away by the error of unprincipled men... ". (2 Peter 3:17)*

Introduction: False teachers were infiltrating the church denying that Christ was the Son of God. This was causing havoc, so Peter penned this letter to bring the people back to the truth of God. He encouraged them to be assured that they had everything they needed for godliness because they had been given the truth and God's precious promises and were partakers of the divine nature of God. They could trust the prophetic Word of God as it was given to them by the Spirit. Peter goes on to identify false teachers and help believers counter the false teacher's claims with the Word of God.

- **Oral Review:** Please refer to the **REVIEW Section** in the following Teaching Guide Outline.

- **Homework:** Review the homework from the book of 1 Peter.

  Review pages 84–85
  Review pages 87–89
  Summarize page 91
  Last question on page 95

- **Review Helps:** Written review is provided at the end of the teacher presentation. (Optional and time permitting.)

- **Teacher Presentation on the Book of Second Peter**

- **Learning for Life:** You may choose to discuss all or just one or two of the questions on page 104.

- **Closing prayer:** Pray that the students will have the spiritual discernment to identify those false teachers that come into their path. Also, pray that they would trust the Bible as the true, inspired Word of God and would stand firm in a godless society.

SECOND PETER
Theme: Identify False Teachers

OUTLINE AID FOR TEACHERS:

I. **CULTIVATION OF CHRISTIAN CHARACTER: TRUE BEHAVIOR (2 PETER 1)**

- **2 Peter 1:3–4**

   A. God has given us everything we need for life and <u>GODLINESS</u>.

      1. God has given us true <u>KNOWLEDGE</u> of God.

      2. God has given us the precious <u>PROMISES</u> of God.

      3. God has made us partakers of the divine <u>NATURE</u> of God.

- **2 Peter 1:5–7**

   B. We are to diligently apply these <u>DIVINE</u> characteristics to our lives:

      1. Moral excellence—living according to God's standard

      2. Knowledge—spiritual knowing; discernment of God's will

      3. Self-Control—strength to handle the pleasures of life (to face good times)

      4. Perseverance—strength to handle the pains of live (to endure bad times)

      5. Godliness—Godlikeness; holiness; being right with God and man

      6. Brotherly kindness (*phileo*)—brotherly love and affection

      7. Love (*agape*)—unconditional love without cause; seeking the welfare of others, not our own

- **2 Peter 1:16–21**

   C. We can trust the prophetic <u>WORD</u> in Scripture.

      1. Peter was an <u>EYEWITNESS</u> to Jesus' majesty and heard the Father speak.

      2. Prophecy did not come from human will but from men moved by God's <u>SPIRIT</u>.

II. **CONDEMNATION OF FALSE TEACHERS: FALSE BEHAVIOR AND FALSE BELIEFS (2 PETER 2)**

- **2 Peter 2:1–3**

   A. False teachers <u>DENY</u> the Master who bought them (no knowledge).

   B. False teachers are <u>SENSUOUS</u>, which gives the way of truth a bad name (no self-control).

   C. False teachers are <u>GREEDY</u> and will exploit people with false words (no love).

D. False teachers indulge in the <u>FLESH</u> (no moral excellence).

- **2 Peter 2:10**

E. False teachers despise <u>AUTHORITY</u> (no godliness).

- **2 Peter 2:14, 17, 19**

F. False teachers <u>ENTICE</u> unstable or new believers (no brotherly kindness).

- **2 Peter 2:20**

G. False teachers <u>KNOW</u> the way of righteousness but turn from it (no perseverance).

III.   COUNTERACTION OF MOCKERS: TRUE BELIEF (2 PETER 3)

- **2 Peter 3:4–10**

A. In order to counter the false, remember the <u>TRUTH</u> spoken by the holy prophets and apostles.

1. Mockers deny Jesus is <u>COMING</u>. The Word says He is.

2. Mockers deny God will <u>JUDGE</u>. The Word says He will.

3. Mockers deny God keeps His <u>PROMISES</u>. The Word says He does.

- **2 Peter 3:11–18**

B. Because Jesus is coming, how should we live?

1. Live <u>GODLY</u> to hasten Jesus' coming.

2. Live <u>GUARDED</u> so error doesn't cause you to fall.

3. Live <u>GROWING</u> in the grace and knowledge of Jesus.

4. Live <u>GLORIFYING</u> our Lord and Savior Jesus Christ!

2 PETER
[Identify False Teachers]

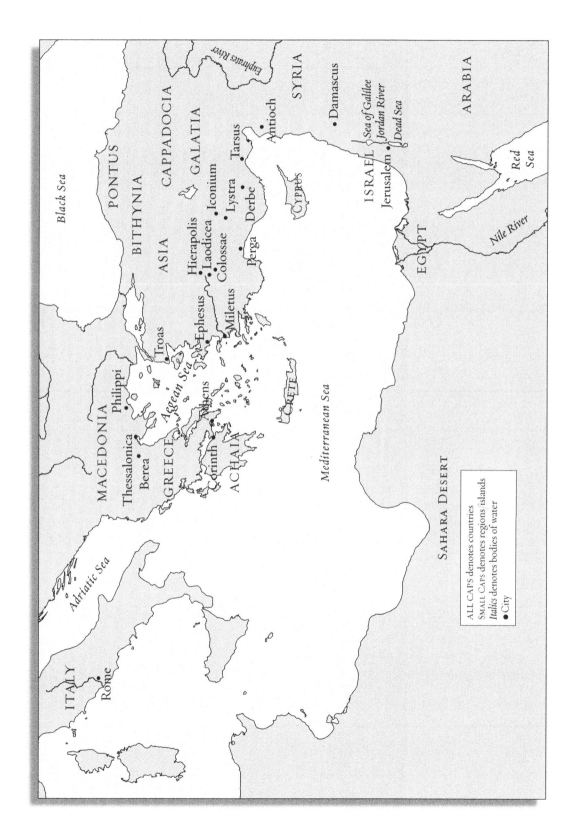

SECOND PETER
Theme: Identify False Teachers

THE BASICS:
⇨ **Who: The Author:** Peter
⇨ **What:** Encouragement to grow in spiritual truth to guard against untruth
⇨ **When:** Written A.D. 64–66
⇨ **Where:** Probably written from Rome to the churches in Asia
⇨ **Why:** To counter false teaching and ungodly behavior in the church

MEMORY VERSE: *"Be on your guard so that you are not carried away by the error of unprincipled men..."* *2 Peter 3:17*

****

REVIEW:

¤ The *Old Testament History* books addressed sin, judgment, and death (the consequences of sin), and the promised Messiah.

¤ The *New Testament History* books addressed Jesus' first coming, His time on earth, and the birth of the church.

¤ In *Paul's Letters to the Churches*, Paul addressed the following:
  ~ **Romans:** God's righteousness described.
  ~ **First Corinthians:** Church's problems corrected.
  ~ **Second Corinthians:** Paul's ministry defended.
  ~ **Galatians:** Believers' freedom in Christ.
  ~ **Ephesians:** Believers' holy walk.
  ~ **Philippians:** Believers' joy in Christ.
  ~ **Colossians:** Believers' completion in Christ.
  ~ **First Thessalonians:** The return of the Lord.
  ~ **Second Thessalonians:** The Day of the Lord.

¤ In *Paul's Letters to Pastors*, Paul addressed the following:
  ~ **First Timothy:** Instructions on leadership.
  ~ **Second Timothy:** Instructions on endurance.
  ~ **Titus:** Instructions on church order.
  ~ **Philemon:** Instructions on forgiveness.

¤ In *Other Letters and Revelation*, the authors addressed:
  ~ **Hebrews:** The superiority of Jesus Christ. The author encouraged the Jewish believers who were suffering for their faith to endure—not to turn back to Judaism. Nothing could compare to what they had in Christ.
  ~ **James:** Addresses true faith—it will have works to prove it.

SECOND PETER
Theme: Identify False Teachers

~ **First Peter:** Speaks to suffering steadfastly—manifesting holiness, harmony, and humility in times of crisis.

OVERVIEW:

****

✳ **ILLUSTRATION:** A woman had just become a Christian and did not have anyone to disciple her, to teach her God's Word. At the time, she was not involved in a Bible study or a church, so she opted to take a correspondence course that lasted four weeks. During this time, she moved to a new neighborhood and was informed that her home was located between two "religious" teachers. The first woman came to her house and stated, "We want to baptize you into our group; but you have to study this book with us first." The woman responded, "What is the book?" The neighbor responded, "Well, it is a book *like* the Bible, but it is additional revelation—greater revelation." The woman, knowing she was a new believer, realized that she knew nothing about God's Word except that Jesus had died for her sins, so she stated, "I don't want to study a book *like* the Bible until I have studied the real thing."

Fortunately, the other neighbor who had also been labeled a "religious" teacher came to visit her shortly after and got her directly into studying the Word of God—*the real thing*!

****

- In the book of 2 Peter, the apostle is concerned about believers' ability to discern between true and false teachers.
- It has been disputed that Peter wrote this book, which is somewhat of a curious thought because the writer gives his name in the greeting:
✝ **2 Peter 1:1** "Simon Peter, a bond-servant and apostle of Jesus Christ, To those who have received a faith of the same kind as ours, by the righteousness of our God and Savior, Jesus Christ ..."
- And the author states that this is his second letter to them:
✝ **2 Peter 3:1** "This is now, beloved, the second letter I am writing to you ..."

- It is not surprising that he referred to himself as "Simon Peter" because he knows that in order to discern truth and error we have to grow in our faith—he was very likely reflecting back to when he was Simon and how he had become Peter the Rock.

- There is a great difference between the writing style of 1 and 2 Peter.
  - ~ It has been said that 1 Peter was written in gloriously smooth Greek.
  - ~ Whereas, 2 Peter is written as though someone was using a Greek dictionary.

SECOND PETER
Theme: Identify False Teachers

- There could be a logical explanation, though.
  - ~ We know that these men dictated their letters, and then signed them.
  - ~ First Peter tells us that Silvanus was the one who wrote down the letter for Peter.
    - ~ Silvanus was a Greek, so he would know the Greek language.
  - ~ Second Peter was apparently written by Peter himself.
    - ~ Peter was a Hebrew, a fisherman who spoke Aramaic—he probably was not that fluent in Greek.
- Why would have Peter written this letter himself? Silvanus must not have been around. But Peter also wrote:
- ✞ **2 Peter 1:14** "... knowing that the laying aside of my earthly dwelling is imminent, as also our Lord Jesus Christ has made clear to me."
  - ~ Peter knew he was about to die.
  - ~ He saw the false teachers coming into the church.
  - ~ Peter felt an urgency to warn the believers in the church to be careful, to be discerning regarding the false teachers.

- In 1 Peter, he had written to encourage the believers to stand firm against the persecution and attacks from those outside the church.

⇨ **The purpose of the book of 2 Peter is to instruct the people on how to identify false teaching within the church and to make them very aware of the dangers of false doctrine.**

I. CULTIVATION OF CHRISTIAN CHARACTER: TRUE BEHAVIOR (2 PETER 1)

- Peter began his letter by clearly acknowledging who Jesus was and is—"our God and Savior, Jesus Christ." (2 Peter 1:1e)

> ★ **TEACHING TIP:**
> *There are those who will state that the Bible does not claim that Jesus is God—Peter with clarity says that Jesus is!*

A. God has given us everything we need for life and GODLINESS.

- ✞ **2 Peter 1:3** "... seeing that His divine power has granted to us everything pertaining to life and godliness, through the true knowledge of Him who called us by His own glory and excellence."

  - Peter was speaking of Jesus' divine power.
  - Through His power, He has provided all that we will ever need for spiritual maturity.
    - ~ But the believer must have the right and true knowledge of Him.

SECOND PETER
Theme: Identify False Teachers

1. God has given us true <u>KNOWLEDGE</u> of God.

- Knowledge of God and faith in Him are the pillars upon which He calls us to live godly lives.
- This comes from knowing His Word—that is the only source of truth or true knowledge.

> ★ **TEACHING TIP:**
> *This is not simply "head" knowledge! It involves "heart" knowledge: faith.*

2. God has given us the precious <u>PROMISES</u> of God.

- He has given these promises in His Word.
- Knowing His promises is vital in living a sanctified life, a life set apart to Him from the world.

> ★ **TEACHING TIP:**
> *Trying to "live like Christ" without having Christ within is unattainable— only a sense of defeat will be achieved.*

3. God has made us partakers of the <u>DIVINE</u> nature of God.

- A believer has God's nature because of the Holy Spirit.

⇨ **The moment a believer asks Jesus into his life, he has everything he will ever need to live a godly life.**

> **NOTE:** Peter said that believers became partakers of the divine nature of God. The apostle Paul referred to this as having the Holy Spirit. They were speaking of the same thing. The Holy Spirit is the power that a believer draws upon.

> ❖ **APPLICATION:** Believers have the Holy Spirit (His divine power) within but often do not draw upon it. As a visual, this is like a person who owns a car with a powerful engine. Instead of using that powerful engine to move the car, the owner gets out of the car and pushes it! That sounds ridiculous, doesn't it?
>
> But believers are very similar to that foolish car owner when they attempt to serve God or respond to others in a godly manner *under their own (human) strength—* instead of appropriating the power that God has provided us!

- A believer has been given power from God.
- Peter went on to state that when Christians have partaken of His divine nature, then they need to cultivate their Christian character.
  - ~ There will be a distinct difference between the behaviors of one with the "true" knowledge of God versus one with "false" knowledge.

B. We are to diligently apply these <u>DIVINE</u> characteristics to our lives:

- Corrie ten Boom was quoted as stating, "The Christian life is not polishing human characteristics but producing divine ones."
- Peter used the word "diligence" in characterizing how believers should approach growing in/applying these virtues to their lives.

> ★ **TEACHING TIP:**
> *A believer does not "add" these virtues—as in "one at a time"—each trait helps and leads into developing the next.*

<u>2 Peter 1:5–7</u>
1. **Moral Excellence—living according to God's standard**
   * Not man's standard, not our own standard, but God's standard.

2. **Knowledge—spiritual knowing; discernment of God's will**
   * The woman in our opening illustration demonstrated discernment—even though she had limited knowledge of God's Word—when she refused to study a book *like* the Bible, but NOT the Bible.

3. **Self-control—strength to handle the pleasures of life (to face good times)**

4. **Perseverance—strength to handle the pains of life (to endure bad times)**

⇨ **A believer needs spiritual strength—God's strength— to handle *both* the good times and the bad times in one's life.**

5. **Godliness—Godlikeness; holiness; being right with God and man**
   * This will lead to the next two character traits.

6. **Brotherly kindness (*phileo*)—brotherly love and affection**

7. **Love (*agape*)—unconditional love without cause; seeking the welfare of others, not our own**

<u>2 Peter 1:8–10b</u>
- Peter explained that if a believer had these qualities—if they were being developed in his life—then two things would become evident:
  ~ A fruitful life.
  ~ Certainty of one's calling by God because of the obvious, striking difference from a worldly character and lifestyle.

- Peter finished his thought process with:

✛ **2 Peter 1:11** "... for in this way the entrance into the eternal kingdom of our Lord and Savior Jesus Christ will be abundantly supplied to you."

~ The terminology of "abundantly supplied" ("abundant entrance") is the same phrase used when the Olympic champions came home from the Olympic Games.

* They would come back to their hometowns or villages to a rich welcome—a triumphant entrance!

> **NOTE:** It seems as if Peter is stating that there are different receptions into heaven.
> - Some, like the winners in the Olympic Games, will experience a celebration.
> - Others will be warmly welcomed, but not the same level of celebration.
>
> - What will make the difference regarding the reception into heaven?
>   ~ Perhaps the difference lies in the believer's diligence in developing these divine characteristics—in seeking to live a holy life as God has called His children to do.
>   ~ Such a believer will experience a triumphant entrance.

> ❖ **APPLICATION:** A good question for each of us to ask ourselves is this: "If I went to heaven today, would they throw a party or am I just going to make it in?"
> ~ An interesting thought to consider.

C. We can trust the prophetic WORD in Scripture.

- Peter gave two reasons as to why believers could have confidence in God's prophetic Word.

2 Peter 1:16–18

1. Peter was an EYEWITNESS to Jesus' majesty and heard the Father speak.

- Peter assured his readers that what he had taught them had not been cleverly devised tales, but he had shared what he had seen with his own eyes.
  ~ Rather it was based on the sharing of historical fact—the truth of the death, burial, and resurrection of Jesus Christ.
- He, in fact, saw with his own two eyes the majesty of Jesus in all His power and glory on the Mount of Transfiguration.

- By what he had directly seen, Peter could testify that Jesus was/is God and He is coming—they could count on this!
- By what he had heard, Peter could attest that God the Father had audibly affirmed that Jesus was His beloved Son with whom He was well pleased—and the Father had said, "Listen to Him [Jesus]!"

2 Peter 1:19–21

2. Prophecy did not come from human will but from men moved by God's SPIRIT.

- Peter gave three points regarding the prophetic Word of God:
  - ~ No prophesy of Scripture can be interpreted by itself—apart from the rest of the Word.
  - ~ No prophesy was ever made by an act of the human will, it was given by the Holy Spirit from God—so it cannot be interpreted by the *natural* mind of man.
  - ~ The Holy Spirit gave the Word to man—the Holy Spirit is the One who Jesus said would teach believers regarding the Word. (John 14:26)

II. CONDEMNATION OF FALSE TEACHERS: FALSE BEHAVIOR AND FALSE BELIEFS (2 PETER 2)

- There is a truism that believers need to remember: one's deeply held beliefs will be revealed in one's behavior—you cannot separate the two. Attitudes will manifest into actions.
- Peter wanted his readers to understand this principle—false doctrines lead to false behavior.
- Peter explained that belief in the truth (God's prophetic Word) produces godly qualities. He begins his next line of thought with a "but":

✞ **2 Peter 2:1** "But false prophets also arose among the people, just as there will also be false teachers among you, ..."

- These believers needed to understand and be prepared for false teachers in their midst—*rising from* among *them*!
- Peter wanted the people to recognize what was happening in their midst:
  - ~ False teachers appear among believers as members of the church.
  - ~ They work secretly—appearing to be what they are not.
  - ~ They bring their false teaching alongside true doctrine, and then ultimately replace the truth with the false.

SECOND PETER
Theme: Identify False Teachers

- Warren Wiersbe makes a great point in his commentary on this passage: *"Please keep in mind that a false teacher is not a person who teaches false doctrine out of ignorance ... False teachers are professed believers who know the truth but who deliberately teach lies in the hope of promoting themselves and getting financial gain from their followers."*

⇨ **It has been said that "heresy" is not merely false doctrine, but it is also false living based on that false doctrine. This is what Peter wanted those in the church to understand.**

2 Peter 2:1–3

A. False teachers <u>DENY</u> the Master who bought them (no knowledge).

- It is important to understand what they are "denying"—the Master who bought them.
  - ~ NOT that Jesus taught them—they had no problem acknowledging that He was a great teacher.
- What were they denying?
  - ~ That Jesus was God who came in the flesh to die and buy us out of sin.
  - ~ Thus, they denied His deity and His sole purpose for coming—salvation.

> ✶ **TEACHING TIP:**
> *Think: there is no need for a Savior if there is no acknowledgement of sin.*

- Because they were "wolves in sheep's clothing," these teachers probably were not overt with their denials but, instead, omitted essential teachings in regards to Jesus and His divinity.

⇨ **The very crux of Christian belief is that Jesus paid the price for the sin debt that all people owed and owe today—in other words, He bought us out of slavery to sin and death.**

- Peter was very clear that the end of such denials would be "destruction"—false teachers will be destroyed.
- Their false doctrine led to false behavior.

B. False teachers are <u>SENSOUS</u>, which gives the way of truth a bad name (no self-control).

C. False teachers are <u>GREEDY</u> and will exploit people with false words (no love).

- Because these teachers denied Christ, their teaching ultimately centered on "self," which led to "self" exaltation.

- ~ They clothed their teaching, however, in religious "speak."
- They often acted on their false doctrine with sinful behavior.
- By doing so, they denigrated the very gospel of Jesus Christ. They practiced sin—what Jesus Christ came to die for.
- False teachers gave a skewed and warped picture of Christianity.

⇨ **The tragic reality is that people will be drawn to such "error" because it omits the subject of "sin"—instead, it embraces and encourages it with "Christian" sounding words.**

> **NOTE:** Peter wanted these believers to demonstrate discernment. Knowing that, an important point must be made: false teachers can use the same words from the Bible as a true teacher would, BUT they use a "different dictionary!"
> - ◆ Their words are false, even if they "sound" biblical.
> - ◆ For example, they may talk about "salvation," but it does not include the fact that we are sinners, that Jesus is God who came in the flesh, that He died on the cross to pay our sin, that He was buried and He rose again, that He ascended into heaven, and that He is coming back.
>   - ~ This is the truth about salvation, but because false teachers deny the Master who bought them, they will add to or subtract from this teaching.
>
> ⇨ **False teachers exploit with their words.**

2 Peter 2:4–9
- Peter gave Old Testament examples to support his teaching—examples of how sin always led to destruction.
  - ~ **Angels**: God did not spare them when they sinned, but He cast them into hell and committed them to the pits of darkness reserved for judgment.
    - ⋆ We do not know exactly who these angels were and when they did this sinning, but we are told very clearly that they are being held in the pit and they will be judged.
    - ⋆ These very well may be the angels mentioned in Revelation 9.
  - ~ **The Ancient World**: God brought a flood on the world of the ungodly.
  - ~ **Sodom and Gomorrah**: God condemned them to destruction by reducing them to ashes, making them an example thereafter to all those who would choose to live ungodly lives.

⇨ **These three illustrations of sin were each followed by destruction from God.**

- In the midst of these examples, Peter gave two illustration of deliverance: Noah and Lot.

✟ **2 Peter 2:5, 7** "... and did not spare the ancient world, but preserved Noah, a preacher of righteousness, with seven others ... and if He rescued righteous Lot, oppressed by the sensual conduct of unprincipled men..."

~ **Noah:** God did not spare the ancient world, but He preserved Noah.
  * For the approximately 120 years that it took Noah to build the ark, he preached righteousness while he worked.
  * Noah told the people to get "right with God"—that they did not have to be destroyed.

~ **Lot:** God rescued Lot because He saw that Lot's soul was tormented day after day by that the attitudes and actions of unprincipled, sinful men.
  * As we learned in the study of Genesis, Abraham gave a choice as to where he would live and Lot chose to live in the area of Sodom and Gomorrah because it was well-watered and because it looked like Eden and the land of Egypt. (Genesis 13:10)
  * He made this choice, even though the area was an ungodly place to live.
  * He also chose to sit by the gate and become one of the leaders of the city.
  * When the angels of God came to tell him of the judgment coming, Lot warned his sons-in-law who did not believe him—rather they thought he was joking.
  * We know that his wife died looking back to Sodom and Gomorrah in their escape.
  * But Lot was saved.

> **✶ TEACHING TIP:**
> *Something to consider: would Lot be a person who did not experience an abundant entrance into heaven? No doubt, God called him righteous— but his own family did not believe what he had to say about God. He lost his wife, who looked back to what she was leaving. It would seem that Lot's walk with God had been inconsistent and not impactful to those he loved.*

D. False teachers indulge in the <u>FLESH</u> (no moral excellence).

****

❋ **ILLUSTRATION:** A Christian speaker had been asked to speak in a foreign country. The hosts put her in a hotel that was located in the middle of the downtown area. Every night at sunset, people would come to the hotel and carouse all night long. At sunrise, they would leave, but return again at sunset. Weeknights, weekends, it did not matter—this was the routine. Sins of all kinds occurred during these nighttime revelries—but always at night ... as if, the dark would "hide" their actions.

****

SECOND PETER
Theme: Identify False Teachers

- Peter stated that the false teacher were so unashamed of their sin that they caroused in the daytime—in the "light" of day ... nothing hidden, all could witness their actions.

- If one's doctrine/beliefs regarding God are wrong, then the consequence is living wrong.

2 Peter 2:10

E. False teachers despise <u>AUTHORITY</u> (no godliness).

- The idea here is that false teachers ascribe to "unbridled freedom," which is solely based on what they think is "right"—leading to an "anything goes" lifestyle.
- They despise the authority of God because they do not want any restraints over their desires or sensual propensities.

2   Peter 2:14a, 17, 19

F.   False teachers <u>ENTICE</u> unstable or new believers (no brotherly kindness).

- The idea behind "entice" is "to bait"—to lure people into a false doctrine that will only lead them AWAY from God—all under the pretense of helping them "find" Him!
  - ~ This included the lost, weak believers, and new believers.

> ★ **TEACHING TIP:**
> *False teachers do not just sin themselves—they want to get others into sinning (as a lifestyle) as well!*

- Paul described their teachings as "springs without water"—they were empty and useless!
- The promises of a false teacher were "empty."
  - ~ To promise freedom, yet be a slave to corruption (dishonesty, exploitation, and fraud), is an empty promise.

G.   False teachers <u>KNOW</u> the way of righteousness but turn from it (no perseverance).

☩ **2 Peter 2:20** "For if, after they have escaped the defilements of the world by the knowledge of the Lord and Savior Jesus Christ, they are again entangled in them and are overcome, the last state has become worse for them than the first."

⇨ **A person cannot lose what he never had, BUT these false teachers HAD the knowledge of salvation—they understood how a person could be saved!**

SECOND PETER
Theme: Identify False Teachers

❖ **APPLICATION:** There are people who come to Bible studies because they have a need or a problem—perhaps they have sinned and feel guilty over it.
  ~ They attend and hear about salvation that promises "freedom," which they find to be a very compelling and attractive message.
  ~ They enjoy hanging around the Christians in the study—they are fun.
  ~ These "new" students even stop sinning, for a period of time, thus becoming free from the guilt that has plagued them.
  ~ BUT there comes a day when they turn from the truth they were learning and turn back to their old ways.

⇨ **Head knowledge—acknowledging God's word as truth—is NOT the same as accepting it as God's truth, which changes the trajectory of one's life.**

- Peter made a bold statement when he said, *"For it would be better for them not to have known the way of righteousness, than having known it, to turn away from the holy commandment handed on to them."* (2 Peter 2:21)

- Peter followed up this statement with two graphic illustrations using dogs and pigs as his examples.
  ~ It is very important to note that he does not use "sheep" (a picture of God's people) in his descriptors. Dogs and pigs were considered "dirty" animals, while sheep were considered "clean."

> ★ **TEACHING TIP:**
> *Peter is NOT talking about true Christians losing their salvation! He is talking about false Christians who never received the divine nature that he addressed in 2 Peter 1:4.*

  1. **Dogs:** When a dog throws up, he is clean on the inside momentarily; but then it returns to its vomit and eats it.
  2. **Pigs:** A pig can be washed on the outside and is clean momentarily, but it eventually will go back and roll in the mud.
  ~ This is the "nature" of these two animals—it is how they internally operate.

- The point of Peter's illustration:
  ~ The animals in his example tried to clean up, but it did not last.
  ~ This is the same for false teachers or those who hear salvation, then turn from it.
    * They try to clean themselves up for a while, but it does not last because they were never truly cleansed from within.

⇨ **Peter has clearly stated that God has given us everything we, as believers, need for a life of godliness—this is permanent, not temporary.**

III. COUNTERACTION OF MOCKERS: TRUE BELIEF (2 PETER 3)

- The word "mockers" is the same Greek word used for "scoffers."
- It speaks to those who will ridicule the truth with a sense of contempt for it as well.
- Remember: these mockers include those who are engaging in a sinful lifestyle.

A. In order to counter the false, remember the <u>TRUTH</u> spoken by the holy prophets and apostles.

- Peter wanted the people to understand that there are three things that false teachers teach that we, as believers, need to know.

1. Mockers deny Jesus is <u>COMING</u>. The Word says He is.

<u>2 Peter 3:4–7</u>

- They basically ask, "What indicators do you have that He is coming? Where is He?"
- Their mocking is based on the argument that nothing has changed since their fathers fell asleep—the world is as it was then. Life moves on just as it did from the beginning.

> **★ TEACHING TIP:**
> *The false conclusion is: why would God break into history now? He never has before.*

- The countering truth is found in verse 5:
- ✝ **2 Peter 3:5–6** "For when they maintain this, it escapes their notice that by the word of God the heavens existed long ago and the earth was formed out of water and by water, through which the world at that time was destroyed, being flooded with water."

- Peter basically stated that they had *purposely* forgotten that the world was destroyed by being flooded with water. They were very familiar with the story of Noah.

> **NOTE:** Why do men have such a hard time believing there was a flood?
> - If a man admits God destroyed the world once—that God judged the world for its sin—then he has to accept the fact that God can do this again.
> - Such acknowledgment presents two choices:
>   1. Change one's life.
>   2. Change God's Word.
> - The false teachers and their followers change God's Word.

2. Mockers deny God will <u>JUDGE</u>. The Word says He will.

- Peter presented a countering truth:

SECOND PETER
Theme: Identify False Teachers

✝ **2 Peter 3:7, 10** "But by His word the present heavens and earth are being reserved for fire, kept for the day of judgment and destruction of ungodly men … But the day of the Lord will come like a thief, in which the heavens will pass away with a roar and the elements will be destroyed with intense heat, and the earth and its works will be burned up."

- In willfully ignoring the truth of the flood and the reason behind it, mockers have no problem scoffing at the idea of God's judgment on the world.
- To accept the concept of "judgment," there must be something that will be judged and the false teachers did NOT (and do not) want to accept the notion that sin will ultimately be judged.

- Another truth was treated with selective amnesia.
    - ~ In Zephaniah, the people were warned that a day of wrath and distress and destruction on men was coming—BECAUSE they had sinned against God. (Zephaniah 1:15, 18)
        - ⋆ This prophecy was very clear that one day the heavens and the earth would be destroyed *by fire*.
- Peter warned that, when God returns to judge, He will come like a thief in the night—unannounced and suddenly.

3. Mockers deny God keeps His <u>PROMISES</u>. The Word says He does.

- Peter reminded his readers:

✝ **2 Peter 3:8-9** "But do not let this one fact escape your notice, beloved, that with the Lord one day is like a thousand years, and a thousand years like one day. The Lord is not slow about His promise, as some count slowness, but is patient toward you, not wishing for any to perish but for all to come to repentance."

- An eternal God does not work on the same "clock" or timetable as temporal man.
- God is not slow—He is patient because His desire is for people to come to repentance, not destruction.
- Peter wanted them to understand that God was giving people time to repent, just as He had given the people 75–100+ years as Noah built the ark and preached repentance.

> ★ **TEACHING TIP:**
>
> *Why is God taking so long? He is giving us time to get right. Aren't you glad that He is patient?*

B. Because Jesus is coming how should we live?

SECOND PETER
Theme: Identify False Teachers

2 Peter 3:11–18

1. Live <u>GODLY</u> to hasten Jesus' coming.

- Live this life knowing that this is not a believer's permanent home—this earth will pass away.
- Look toward Christ's coming—and our eternal home.
- While awaiting His return, live in peace, spotless, and blameless—be a living testimony to God.

2. Live <u>GUARDED</u> so error doesn't cause you to fall.

- *Be aware* and *beware* of those who would teach error, leading people away from God.
- Understand that there are those in your midst—in your local church—who could deceive you with false teaching.
- Live guarded—be discerning of what you hear and see—in order to remain steadfast in standing on God's truth.

3. Live <u>GROWING</u> in the grace and knowledge of Jesus.

- Grow *forward* in knowing Jesus—do not go backward, away from Him.
- Know God's Word yourself so that you can be discerning.
- Cultivate His Word in every aspect of your life.

4. Live <u>GLORIFYING</u> our Lord and Savior Jesus Christ!

- If a believer is growing, he will glorify God.
- What does it mean to "glorify" God?
    - ~ It is to give a correct picture of who Jesus is.
    - ~ It is accomplished by how we live—our words, our actions, our attitudes—how we relate to God and others.

FINAL THOUGHTS AND APPLICATION

- Peter warned believers that false teachers were coming and that they would come from within the church.

- Peter wanted the people to wake up to this fact, to be alert and on guard to what was taught as truth.

- He did not want any believer to fall for the lies of false teaching because the truth remains that:

~   Jesus is coming.

~   He is coming to judge.

~   He keeps all of His promises.

❖ **FINAL APPLICATION:** **Are you growing in the truth of God's Word so you can discern the false teachers around you today?**

SECOND PETER REVIEW HELPS

✧ Write out as many lessons as you have learned from _Other Letters and Revelation_, beginning with Hebrews. As people who were living under extreme persecution, how do you think these letters would have brought them comfort?

You may use your Bibles. Discuss your answers as a group.

FIRST JOHN

Fellowship with God

By this we know that we have come to know Him,

if we keep His commandments.

1 John 2:3

SESSION SIXTY-TWO: FIRST JOHN
Fellowship with God

✝ **Memory verse:** *By this we know that we have come to know Him, if we keep His commandments. (1 John 2:3)*

Introduction: John was an eyewitness to the works and life of Jesus Christ. Now sixty years later, as an aged man, he wanted believers to understand clearly that in Jesus is life, light, and love. The Gnostics were making inroads into the faith, preaching that knowledge was superior to virtue. But John emphasizes the reality of the incarnation and the changed life that comes with high moral and ethical standards. Because of their love for God, believers should live in obedience to Him. Obedience proves the believers' love.

- **Oral Review:** Please refer to the **REVIEW Section** in the following Teaching Guide Outline.

- **Homework:** Review the homework from the book of 2 Peter.

    Review pages 109–110
    Review page 112
    Review page 115
    Review pages 118–119

- **Review Helps:** Written review is provided at the end of the teacher presentation. (Optional and time permitting.)

- **Teacher Presentation on the Book of First John**

- **Learning for Life:** You may choose to discuss all or just one or two of the questions on page 127.

- **Closing prayer:** Pray that, through this little book, they will grow more in love with Christ and more in love with one another. Pray that their faith would be a beacon of light to non-believers, their love of one another would bring unity in the church, and their life would be an example of Christ to their family, their community, and the world.

FIRST JOHN
Theme: Fellowship with God

OUTLINE AID FOR TEACHERS:

I. **INTRODUCTION TO 1 JOHN (1 JOHN 1:1–4)**

II. **WALKING IN GOD'S LIGHT (1 JOHN 1:5–2:29)**

- **1 John 1:5–10**

  A. We will <u>CONFESS</u> our sins.

- **1 John 2:3–6**

  B. We will <u>OBEY</u> God's commandments.

- **1 John 2:7–11**

  C. We will <u>LOVE</u> one another.

- **1 John 2:15–17**

  D. We will not love the <u>WORLD</u>.

      1. Lust of the <u>FLESH</u>

      2. Lust of the <u>EYES</u>

      3. Pride of <u>LIFE</u>

- **1 John 2:18–29**

  E. We will avoid <u>FALSE</u> teachers.

III. **WALKING IN GOD'S LOVE (1 JOHN 3–4)**

- **1 John 3:1–3**

  A. He has made us His <u>CHILDREN</u>.

- **1 John 3:4, 8–9**

      1. Satan's children are obvious.

          a. They practice <u>SIN</u>.

          b. They do not <u>LOVE</u> others.

- **1 John 3:16–18**

  B. Christ is our <u>EXAMPLE</u> of love.

      1. Love is <u>SACRIFICIAL</u>.

      2. Love is <u>ACTION</u>.

FIRST JOHN
Theme: Fellowship with God

- **1 John 3:22–4:13**

  C. There are <u>BENEFITS</u> of being God's children.

    1. We have answered <u>PRAYER</u>.

    2. We have the indwelling of the <u>HOLY SPIRIT</u>.

    3. We have confidence on the Day of <u>JUDGMENT</u>.

IV. **WALKING IN GOD'S LIFE (1 JOHN 5)**

- **1 John 5:4**

  A. Through Jesus Christ we have <u>VICTORY</u> over the world.

- **1 John 5:6b, 10**

  B. Through Jesus Christ we have the <u>WITNESS</u> of the Spirit.

- **1 John 5:11–12**

  C. Through Jesus Christ we have <u>ETERNAL LIFE</u>.

- **1 John 5:14–15**

  D. Through Jesus Christ we know God <u>HEARS</u> our prayers.

- **1 John 5:18**

  E. Through Jesus Christ we have <u>PROTECTION</u> from Satan.

I John
[Fellowship with God]

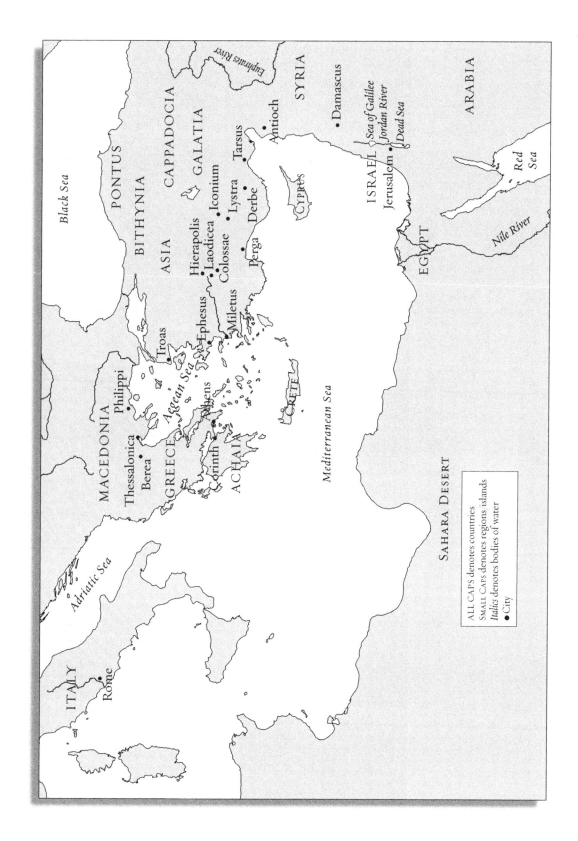

ALL CAPS denotes countries
SMALL CAPS denotes regions/islands
Italics denotes bodies of water
• City

FIRST JOHN
Theme: Fellowship with God

THE BASICS:

⇨ **Who: The Author:** John

⇨ **What:** A letter written to encourage believers in their fellowship with God and one another

⇨ **When:** Written around A.D. 90

⇨ **Where:** Probably written from Ephesus to the churches in Asia

⇨ **Why:** False teachers were threatening sound doctrine

MEMORY VERSE: *"By this we know that we have come to know Him, if we keep His commandments." 1 John 2:3*

****

REVIEW:

⌘ The *Old Testament History* books addressed sin, judgment, and death (the consequences of sin), and the promised Messiah.

⌘ The *New Testament History* books addressed Jesus' first coming, His time on earth, and the birth of the church.

⌘ In *Paul's Letters to the Churches*, Paul addressed the following:
  ~ **Romans:** God's righteousness described.
  ~ **First Corinthians:** Church's problems corrected.
  ~ **Second Corinthians:** Paul's ministry defended.
  ~ **Galatians:** Believers' freedom in Christ.
  ~ **Ephesians:** Believers' holy walk.
  ~ **Philippians:** Believers' joy in Christ.
  ~ **Colossians:** Believers' completion in Christ.
  ~ **First Thessalonians:** The return of the Lord.
  ~ **Second Thessalonians:** The Day of the Lord.

⌘ In *Paul's Letters to Pastors*, Paul addressed the following:
  ~ **First Timothy:** Instructions on leadership.
  ~ **Second Timothy:** Instructions on endurance.
  ~ **Titus:** Instructions on church order.
  ~ **Philemon:** Instructions on forgiveness.

⌘ In *Other Letters and Revelation*, the authors addressed:
  ~ **Hebrews:** Christ's superiority.
  ~ **James:** Live faith through works.
  ~ **First Peter:** Suffering steadfastly.

FIRST JOHN
Theme: Fellowship with God

~ **Second Peter**: Identifying false teachers—the danger of error coming from within the church.

OVERVIEW:

- This little book was written by the apostle John.
- In 1 John, the author points out three aspects of the living God:
  1. God is light
  2. God is love
  3. God is life
- John taught these three characteristics that explained why and how Christian fellowship is so very different from the world's definition of fellowship.

****

❋ **ILLUSTRATION:** A woman recalled the first time, at age thirty-two, when she experienced the company of women who loved God and loved Jesus Christ: "First of all, I was overcome because they truly seemed to love me and I wasn't particularly that loveable. They laughed a lot. They had a good time together, but it was a different kind of fun—it was clean fun."

"The other thing that I just found so wonderful is that they were a safe harbor. I could be with them and feel comfortable, but I knew that, once I left, they weren't going to talk about me behind my back. I knew that because when I was with them they did not talk about other women who were not present. So it didn't matter if you were physically with them or not, they were a safe harbor. They would not talk about you, they would not judge you, they were not 'catty.' It was absolutely awe-inspiring to me that such a community existed. It was my introduction to the great love of Jesus Christ."

****

- This is the first of three letters John wrote.
- The word "love" is mentioned over thirty-five times.
- John also wrote this book in "contrasts":
  ~ Light with darkness
  ~ Truth with error
  ~ God with the devil
  ~ Righteousness with sin
  ~ Love with hate
  ~ Life with death

FIRST JOHN
Theme: Fellowship with God

- John was an interesting man:
  - ~ More has been written about him than any of the other disciples.
    He was the one disciple who lived to a ripe old age and died of natural causes.
  - ~ He was the disciple who was with Jesus at all of the really important events that took place during His ministry.
  - ~ He came to Christ probably through John the Baptist.
    - ⋆ He was most likely intrigued with John the Baptist and listened to his teaching.
    - ⋆ It seemed that he knew John the Baptist was pointing to a Messiah.
    - ⋆ He was business partners with James (his brother), Peter, and Andrew as fishermen—they all joined Jesus about the same time.
    - ⋆ John was the one disciple that was present at the crucifixion.
    - ⋆ He took Jesus' mother into his own home and cared for her until her death.

⇨ **Given this background, John held a very important place in Christian history.**

- John wrote five books of the Bible:
  - ~ Gospel of John
  - ~ First John, 2 John, and 3 John
  - ~ Book of Revelation
- There is no doubt that John has contributed greatly to our Christian heritage and doctrine.

⇨ **The purpose of 1 John is to explain what fellowship with God involves: walking in His light, walking in His love, and walking in His life.**

NOTE TO TEACHER: This is a hard book to outline.
So be aware that you will find the material going along in one direction,
and then coming back to material you have already covered.

I.   INTRODUCTION TO 1 JOHN (1 JOHN 1:1–4)

- First John does not have a formal greeting—there is no salutation. There are no people mentioned in this book.
  - ~ Very different from the other epistles in the New Testament.
- Instead, John began his letter with the truth about the Word—Jesus was/is the incarnate Word. (John 1:1)
  - ⋆ He saw, heard, and touched Jesus.
  - ⋆ He experienced fellowship with Jesus.
  - ⋆ He wanted the readers to experience the same fellowship with Jesus Christ.

FIRST JOHN
Theme: Fellowship with God

- John was setting the stage for exposing and addressing wrong doctrine. At that time, Gnostics were stirring up trouble among the Christian faith (parts of it are still a battle for believers).

- What did the Gnostics teach?
  - **Dualism:**
    - Stated that the spirit was good, but matter was evil—and the two were separate from one another.
    - Thus a man's body was evil, but his spirit was good. In other words, the body was not responsible for what it did because it was evil (i.e., it could not help itself).
    - And because a man's spirit was good (and separate from his body), it would go on to heaven no matter what the man indulged in with his body.
    - The end result? Immorality was rampant.
  - **The Resurrection:**
    - It was not really God who was part of the resurrection.
    - They taught that Jesus was born an ordinary man and He lived an ordinary life until the day He was baptized.
    - They further taught that when Jesus was baptized, God came into Jesus to dwell with Him. This "indwelling" continued until just before the crucifixion.
    - Gnostics taught that it was a human, not God, who was crucified.
  - **Mysteries of Faith:**
    - They taught that there were mysteries that only a few people could understand—these were the chosen ones who would alone go to heaven.
    - To them everything was secret and these little secret ideas were only given to a few.
  - The Gnostic teachings were vastly different from Christian doctrine, yet they were infiltrating the church.

II. WALKING IN GOD'S LIGHT (1JOHN 1:5–2:29)

- The Gnostics taught that things about God were "hidden"—they were "secret."
- John responded with a resounding, "Not true!"

✝ **1 John 1:5** "This is the message we have heard from Him and announce to you, that God is Light, and in Him there is no darkness at all."

- John explained that, when a person walked with God, everything was revealed because they were walking IN the light.

FIRST JOHN
Theme: Fellowship with God

- His point to believers:
  - ~ God is present: *He is with you all the time.*
  - ~ God is light: *in this, all things—our obedience and disobedience—are revealed.*

> ❖ **APPLICATION:** This might well be considered double-edged sword "good" news!
> - ~ If we are walking in obedience, we love knowing that Jesus is with us 24/7.
> - ~ But, if we are walking in disobedience, we prefer the "dark," not wanting God to see our sin.

A. We will CONFESS our sins.

1 John 1:5–10

- As we walk in God's light, we must confess our sins because He is righteous and will forgive our sins.
- John wanted believers to understand that God offered a continual cleansing of sin—such as: if they did or said or thought something that was against what God would have His children do.
- When believers sin they have the great privilege of being able to go to the Father, confess, be cleansed of it, and continue walking in the light.

> **NOTE:** If we obey God, we walk in the light. If we disobey God, we walk in darkness.
> - ◆ God is light—Satan is the prince of darkness.
>
> - ⇨ **Fellowship will be based on the realm in which we choose to walk: light or darkness.**

B. We will OBEY God's commandments.

1 John 2:3–6

- Obedience to God is the outflow of having fellowship with Him—it is the "marker" that we know Him, that we are His.
- Christians do and will sin—this will break our fellowship with God, but not our "sonship."

C. We will LOVE one another.

1 John 2:7–11

- A trait demonstrating that a person knows God and is His child is a love for fellow believers.

FIRST JOHN
Theme: Fellowship with God

✝ **1 John 2:10a** "The one who loves his brother abides in the Light …"

> ■ John was simply reiterating the point Jesus had made regarding love:

✝ **John 13:35** "By this all men will know that you are My disciples, if you have love for one another."

> ■ John understood the power of love—he had experienced it in his fellowship with Jesus.
>
> ■ He wanted these believers to understand the connection between God's love and light:
> > ~ When believers actively practice love toward other believers, Christ's light shines through them because such love is not natural.
> > > ★ This love is neither selective nor prejudicial in nature, but is unconditional in its giving and asks nothing in return—such love is a "foreign" concept to the world.

> ★ **TEACHING TIP:**
> *Not only are believers to walk in the Light but they are to "abide" in the Light. Believers need to "remain in" or "continue in" the Light—love will be the fruit.*

D. We will not love the <u>WORLD</u>.

■ A second trait of believers who are walking in God's Light is that they will not love the things of the world, things that would draw attention and devotion away from Jesus Christ.

■ The "world" refers to anything and everything that belongs to "this" life that opposes Jesus Christ.

■ What will draw us away from Jesus and make it "easy" for us to sin?
> ~ Satan used all three in the Garden.

1 John 2:15–16

> 1. **Lust of the <u>FLESH</u>.**
>   > ★ This involves indulging in a "fleshly" pleasure.
>   > ★ Anything that a person could do or use that would alter their devotion to Jesus and desire to walk in His light.
>   > ★ Examples: sexual immorality, gluttony, or drunkenness.
>
> 2. **Lust of the <u>EYES</u>.**
>   > ★ The eyes delight in things that a person cannot have.
>   > ★ This would include coveting and jealousy.

❖ **APPLICATION:** Have you experienced this at your local mall? Be honest!
  ~ You're at home, exhibiting no problems with the "lust of the eyes …"
  ~ And then you head to the mall and begin to see things you "want" but cannot afford …
  ~ You see others buying all those things you now "need" (actually still a "want") …
  ~ You feel a tinge of jealousy that somehow leads to coveting that turns into anger because you can't have what you want!

---

3. Pride of <u>LIFE</u>.
  * This is when we want to be like God—we want to be the little "g" god of our own life.
  * This is a desire for control, for admiration and praise.

- If these three traits consistently and habitually characterize a person's life, then he or she is not walking in the Light and does not love God or those who belong to Him.

E. We will avoid <u>FALSE</u> teachers.

<u>1 John 2:18–29</u>
- This instruction/warning was shared over and over again by John and other New Testament writers.
- John told the people that these false teachers:
  ~ Were no longer in fellowship with true believers—they had gone out from them revealing that they were not really of them.
  ~ Denied that Jesus was the Christ, incarnate God.
  ~ Tried to deceive those in the church—lure them away from the truth.
- John encouraged the people to abide in (remain in) Jesus Christ and actively practice His righteousness as a lifestyle.
  ~ False teachers do not practice God's righteousness nor do they encourage it.

III. WALKING IN GOD'S LOVE (1 JOHN 3–4)

A. He has made us His <u>CHILDREN</u>.

<u>1 John 3:1–3</u>
- Believers are children of the King!
- When a believer came to faith in Christ, he or she stepped over into a new kingdom.
  ~ Believers are part of God's family.
  ~ Believers are called to walk in love because God is love.

FIRST JOHN
Theme: Fellowship with God

- John made the case that the actions and attitudes of a child of God distinguish him from others.

  ## 1. Satan's children are obvious.

  <u>1 John 3:4, 8–9</u>
  ### a. They practice <u>SIN</u>.

  - ⋆ The word "practice" indicates a deliberate, habitual action in disobeying God.
  - ⋆ There is also the sense that Satan's children do not care about what they are doing (sinning against God and others) or its impact on others.
  - ⋆ The children of Satan sin and enjoy it.

  ### b. They do not <u>LOVE</u> others.

  - ⋆ They also have no love for one another or others.
  - ⋆ This lack of love is a distinct character trait in the children of Satan—it distinguishes them from God's children.

  NOTE: There are many who view Satan as some kind of caricature that does not really exist—that he is not a foe or enemy. This is what the "deceiver" would like people to believe, but it is a lie. Satan does exist and he is God's enemy, a believer's greatest opponent.
  - His very name, Satan, is mentioned thirty-six times in the New Testament.
  - The word "devil" is mentioned thirty-three times.
  - He is a very powerful angel—a created being.
  - He is smart and powerful.
  - He is not omnipresent, but has many demons doing his bidding.
  - His evil focus is on anyone who is for Jesus Christ.
  - Some of the names for Satan are the:

    - ~ Destroyer
    - ~ Accuser of the brethren
    - ~ Adversary
    - ~ Deceiver of the whole world
    - ~ Evil one
    - ~ God or ruler of this world
    - ~ Liar
    - ~ Murderer
    - ~ Tempter

  - He is the one responsible for the great self-centeredness of the nations.
  - He deceives the political world.
  - He has godless ideologies that impact the masses of humanity.
  - The whole "natural" world is in his power.
  - He will use the weakness of a man/woman to tempt him/her—to lure them to all that is worldly.

FIRST JOHN
Theme: Fellowship with God

- In 1 John, the apostle John told the people to "beware" and "be aware" of their foe, Satan. He did not want them to be ignorant on this subject.

B. Christ is our <u>EXAMPLE</u> of love.

1. Love is <u>SACRIFICIAL</u>.

✟ **1 John 3:16** "We know love by this, that He laid down His life for us; and we ought to lay down our lives for the brethren."

- In 1 Corinthians 13 we were given traits of what God defined as "love."
  - ~ The characteristics within this chapter run contrary in many ways to how the world represents "love."
  - ~ The love that God calls us to live out can only be accomplished as the Holy Spirit of God loves through us.
- Here in 1 John 3:16, John gave an example of love, not the characteristics.
  - ~ Love "laid down His life" for others.
- John called believers to follow Jesus' example.

> ✶ **TEACHING TIP:**
> *In remembering that Jesus hung on the cross for agonizing hours because He loved us, we need to answer the call to "extra mile" love—helping others, caring for others when we may not "feel" like we have the time or energy because Jesus so loved us.*

2. Love is <u>ACTION</u>.

- This involves giving of one's time, care, goods, and prayers.

✟ **1 John 3:18** "Little children, let us not love with word or with tongue, but in deed and truth."

****

✷ **ILLUSTRATION:** There was a woman whose mother was dying of cancer. She was a daughter, but also a wife and mother—trying her best to juggle all three roles. She was exhausted and grieving over a loss she knew was coming. Two women (sisters in Christ) saw her plight and acted. The first woman started picking up her children after school each day, so that the woman could stay by her mother's side. She essentially gave a daughter "time" to love her mother in her last days.

When the mother died, the second woman stepped in. Household chores had fallen through the cracks. So, while the family gathered at another family member's house, she cleaned the woman's house, as if it belonged to Jesus Himself. Every nook and cranny, the toilets, the dirty dishes in the sink, the laundry—the house simply shone!

FIRST JOHN
Theme: Fellowship with God

When the daughter walked into her home that evening, she wept over the love that she felt from both of these women—who had given of their time and selves, expecting nothing in return. She had experienced the love of Christ through these two believers. They demonstrated God's love in action—"in deed and truth."

****

> ❖ **APPLICATION:** Have you ever responded to a need as the two women in the illustration? Often we will tell someone who is hurting, "I am so sorry—I will pray for you." Prayer is needed, but love also acts!
> ~ It is easy to "speak" love, but what Christ did on the cross was love in action.
> ~ We must be willing to be free and generous with our love for one another.

C. There are <u>BENEFITS</u> of being God's children.

1. We have answered <u>PRAYER</u>.

✝ **1 John 3:22** "… and whatever we ask we receive from Him, because we keep His commandments and do the things that are pleasing in His sight."

2. We have the indwelling of the <u>HOLY SPIRIT</u>.

✝ **1 John 4:13** "By this we know that we abide in Him and He in us, because He has given us of His Spirit."

- It is the Spirit of God, the Holy Spirit, who convicts us of sin.
- It is the Holy Spirit who comforts us when we are hurting.
- He is the One who encourages the believer.
- How? By bringing Scriptures to mind—by reminding us of God's Word, His promises.

3. We have confidence on the Day of <u>JUDGMENT</u>.

✝ **1 John 4:17** "By this, love is perfected with us, so that we may have confidence in the day of judgment; because as He is, so also are we in this world."

- In 1 Corinthians, we learned about the day when believers will stand before the Lord—this is the bema seat. It is not for unbelievers, only for believers.
- When believers stand before the Lord, they are not judged as to whether they are saved or unsaved, whether they belong to Christ or not.
- Believers belong to Christ, so eternal life with Him is sure.
- Believers will be judged on "works."
  - ~ Good works will remain because they were made out of gold and silver.
  - ~ Worthless works will burn up.

FIRST JOHN
Theme: Fellowship with God

- John wanted these believers to know that they would be safe on the Day of Judgment because they belonged to Christ, they were His.

REVIEW:

- John called the church to walk in God's Light.
  - ~ He exhorted them to be clean, pure, confident, and obedient.
- He called them to walk in God's love.
  - ~ In doing so, the love of Christ could flow through them to others.

  - John ended his letter by calling the people to walk in the life of God.

IV. WALKING IN GOD'S LIFE (1 JOHN 5)

A. Through Jesus Christ we have __VICTORY__ over the world.

✝ **1 John 5:4** "For whatever is born of God overcomes the world; and this is the victory that has overcome the world — our faith."

  - A believer has the Spirit of God within—His power can bring victory in a believer's life.

****

❋ **ILLUSTRATION:** There was a believer who had been a prodigal. He had come to the Lord early in life, then strayed into alcoholism. But he had returned to the Lord in repentance and sought to stay on the road to sobriety. A series of difficult events entered his life and he began to be tempted to escape from his problems by going back into the "bottle."

Something deep within moved him to open his Bible. His eyes fell upon 1 John 5:4—he realized that the Spirit was reminding him that he was an "overcomer" and to hold on to his faith, not a bottle! This was a turning point in his life and his road to full sobriety. He never looked to alcohol again because he knew who he was as a child of God—an overcomer who could live in victory because of Jesus!

****

  - The world and Satan will try to lead a believer astray but, because we have the Spirit of God within, we can experience victory!

B. Through Jesus Christ we have the __WITNESS__ of the Spirit.

✝ **1 John 5:6b, 10** "… It is the Spirit who testifies, because the Spirit is the truth … The one who believes in the Son of God has the testimony in himself; the one who does not believe

FIRST JOHN
Theme: Fellowship with God

God has made Him a liar, because he has not believed in the testimony that God has given concerning His Son."

- One of the works of the Spirit is to help a believer discern that which is good and that which is evil—that which is true and that which is false.

C. Through Jesus Christ we have ETERNAL LIFE.

✠ **1 John 5:11–12** "And the testimony is this, that God has given us eternal life, and this life is in His Son. He who has the Son has the life; he who does not have the Son of God does not have the life."

- Eternal life is found in Jesus Christ—God has given witness to this truth.

D. Through Jesus Christ we know God HEARS our prayers.

✠ **1 John 5:14–15** "This is the confidence which we have before Him, that, if we ask anything according to His will, He hears us. And if we know that He hears us in whatever we ask, we know that we have the requests which we have asked from Him."

- Consider this: the God of the entire universe, the Creator of everything, He who is high and lifted up—He hears your prayers!
- When we pray in His will, we can pray with confidence (boldness).

⇨ **Confidence comes when we have the life of God within and we are living and walking in the life of God!**

E. Through Jesus Christ we have PROTECTION from Satan.

✠ **1 John 5:18** "We know that no one who is born of God sins; but He who was born of God keeps him, and the evil one does not touch him."

- This verse is *not* saying that Christians do not sin! It IS saying that believers do not "practice" sin. In other words, they do not habitually, knowingly, live in sin.
- To have the promised victory in Christ a believer must yield to Christ—but there will be spiritual warfare in seeking to live in obedience.
- Through Jesus Christ, a believer has protection from Satan.

✠ **1 John 5:20** "And we know that the Son of God has come, and has given us understanding so that we may know Him who is true; and we are in Him who is true, in His Son Jesus Christ. This is the true God and eternal life."

FIRST JOHN
Theme: Fellowship with God

- Believers are "aliens" living on earth—we are citizens in the kingdom of God.
- But as "aliens" we can walk confidently in God's light, in His love, and in the life that He offers for all eternity.

FINAL THOUGHTS AND APPLICATION

- At the time that John wrote this letter he was a very old man. He had walked with Christ for a long time.
- As a young man, John had been called the "Son of Thunder"—probably because he was an angry man.
  - This is hard for us to believe today because we consider him as a man who was tender-hearted, gentle-spirited, and full of love.
- John changed through the years, through the work of Christ in his life, through walking in Christ's light and love.
- John wanted believers to understand the life—the victorious life—that was possible in and through Jesus Christ.

- ❖ **FINAL APPLICATION:** Do those around you see your love for God by the way you love others?

FIRST JOHN
Theme: Fellowship with God

FIRST JOHN REVIEW HELPS

✧ Give each table cards with the names of the books that have already been studied. Have the tables work together to review the themes of those books. Give them about ten minutes to do so. Then, starting in Genesis, have the people who have the cards give a two-sentence summary of the book. Go through all sixty-one books.

SECOND JOHN

Shun False Teachers

If anyone comes to you and does not bring this teaching,

do not receive him into your house.

2 John 10

SESSION SIXTY-THREE: SECOND JOHN
Shun False Teachers

✝ **Memory verse:** *"If anyone comes to you and does not bring this teaching, do not receive him into your house." (2 John 10)*

Introduction: In 1 John, he admonished the believers to walk in light, love, and life. In this little epistle, he encourages them to also walk in truth. He again emphasizes the command to love one another and, once more, the problem with false teachers was addressed.

- **Oral Review:** Please refer to the **REVIEW Section** in the following Teaching Guide Outline.

- **Homework:** Review the homework from the book of 1 John.

    Questions in the middle and bottom of page 132
    Review pages 135–136
    Review pages 137–139

- **Review Helps:** Written review is provided at the end of the teacher presentation. (Optional and time permitting.)

- **Teacher Presentation on the Book of Second John**

- **Learning for Life:** You may choose to discuss all or just one or two of the questions on page 151.

- **Closing prayer:** Pray that students would know the truth and that truth would set them free and that freedom would result in greater love for God and greater love for one another.

SECOND JOHN
Theme: Shun False Teachers

OUTLINE AID FOR TEACHERS:

I. **JOHN COMMENDED HIS RECIPIENTS FOR WALKING IN THE TRUTH (2 JOHN 1–4)**

   A. John's greeting expressed love for those knowing and <u>PRACTICING</u> the truth.

   B. John understood that abiding truth is <u>ETERNAL</u>.

   C. It pleased John to learn that some children were living in <u>OBEDIENCE</u>.

II. **JOHN COMMANDED HIS RECIPIENTS TO LOVE ONE ANOTHER (2 JOHN 5–6)**

   A. John's letter was a reminder to live out the <u>COMMANDMENT</u> to love.

   B. John defined love as <u>OBEDIENCE</u> to Christ's commandment.

III. **JOHN CAUTIONED HIS RECIPIENTS TO WATCH OUT FOR FALSE TEACHERS (2 JOHN 7–13)**

   A. John warned about deceivers who denied Jesus' <u>COMING</u>.

   B. John cautioned his recipients to not lose what has been <u>GAINED</u>.

   C. John stated that Christian teaching must include <u>CHRIST</u> or the teacher is without God.

   D. John commanded that those who come with false teaching must neither be <u>RECEIVED</u> nor <u>GREETED</u>.

   E. John further stated that if a false teacher was offered hospitality, the host would be <u>GUILTY</u> of participating in evil.

   F. John ended with the hope of personally <u>DELIVERING</u> the next message.

2 JOHN
[Shun False Teachers]

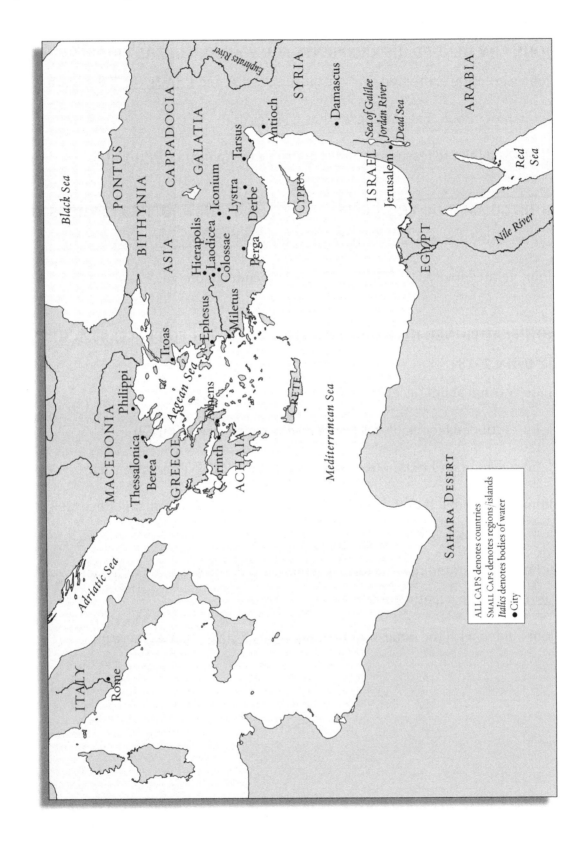

SECOND JOHN
Theme: Shun False Teachers

THE BASICS:

⇨ **Who: The Author:** John

⇨ **What:** A teaching on walking in truth

⇨ **When:** Written around A.D. 90

⇨ **Where:** Written from Ephesus to a believing woman and her child or a church and its members

⇨ **Why:** To applaud obedience to the truth and warn against false teachers

MEMORY VERSE: *"If anyone comes to you and does not bring this teaching, do not receive him into your house."* *2 John 10*

****

REVIEW:

⌑ The *Old Testament History* books addressed sin, judgment, and death (the consequences of sin), and the promised Messiah.

⌑ The *New Testament History* books addressed Jesus' first coming, His time on earth, and the birth of the church.

⌑ In *Paul's Letters to the Churches*, Paul addressed the following:
  ~ **Romans:** God's righteousness described.
  ~ **First Corinthians:** Church's problems corrected.
  ~ **Second Corinthians:** Paul's ministry defended.
  ~ **Galatians:** Believers' freedom in Christ.
  ~ **Ephesians:** Believers' holy walk.
  ~ **Philippians:** Believers' joy in Christ.
  ~ **Colossians:** Believers' completion in Christ.
  ~ **First Thessalonians:** The return of the Lord.
  ~ **Second Thessalonians:** The Day of the Lord.

⌑ In *Paul's Letters to Pastors*, Paul addressed the following:
  ~ **First Timothy:** Instructions on leadership.
  ~ **Second Timothy:** Instructions on endurance.
  ~ **Titus:** Instructions on church order.
  ~ **Philemon:** Instructions on forgiveness.

⌑ In *Other Letters and Revelation*, the authors addressed:
  ~ **Hebrews:** Christ's superiority.
  ~ **James:** Live faith through works.
  ~ **First Peter:** Suffering steadfastly.

SECOND JOHN
Theme: Shun False Teachers

- ~ **Second Peter**: Identify false teachers.
- ~ **First John:** Experiencing true fellowship with God—walking in His light, His love, and His life.

OVERVIEW:

- Have you ever been fooled by anything fake? Technology has reached the ability to make things look real that are not—in fact, technology can make things look better than the real.
  - ~ Perhaps you have seen a beautiful flower, only to realize that it is artificial when you tried to smell its fragrance.

****

- ❋ **ILLUSTRATION:** There was a woman who was standing before her mirror one evening as she was preparing to go to bed. As she stood in front of that mirror, she began to remove things.
  - ~ First, her hairpiece that made her short hair look long … that went into a drawer.
  - ~ Then her long, curly eyelashes … they went into the drawer.
  - ~ Then her baby blue contact lenses that made her eyes the color she wanted them to be … they went into the drawer.
  - ~ Then she removed the "beauty mole" that she had attached to her face … it went into the drawer.
  - ~ Then she removed the little dental piece that made the space between her two front teeth disappear … it went into the drawer.
  - ~ Then she removed the body-enhancing equipment that added and subtracted to her natural physique.
  - ~ Then she removed her makeup that gave her the appearance of a flawless complexion … underneath the flaws were evident.

The woman looked at the reflection in the mirror—with all the manufactured pieces of disguise and enhancements placed in a drawer—and she saw her true appearance.

Her husband had watched this scene play out and said to his wife as she headed to bed, "I am not really sure if I need to climb in bed or in that drawer."

****

- False teaching and untruths were very prevalent when John penned this second letter. Just like the woman in the illustration, the truth was being altered with counterfeit additions.
- John wanted the people to understand the importance of knowing the truth, so that they could recognize when an untruth or false doctrine was being presented.

SECOND JOHN
Theme: Shun False Teachers

- He did not want believers fooled by any teaching that "appeared" like the truth but wasn't.

- John was probably ninety years old when he wrote this letter. He was living in Ephesus.
- He wrote the people to applaud their obedience to Christ, as well as warn them about the false teaching in their midst.

- Second John is the second-shortest book in the Bible—the shortest being 3 John by one line.

⇨ **The purpose of 2 John was to instruct believers to shun false teachers—holding tightly to the true Word of God and refusing to listen to or fellowship with anyone who would alter it.**

I. JOHN COMMENDED HIS RECIPIENTS FOR WALKING IN THE TRUTH (2 JOHN 1–4)

A. John's greeting expressed love for those knowing and PRACTICING the truth.

✞ **2 John 1** "The elder to the chosen lady and her children whom I love in truth; and not only I, but also all who know the truth ..."

- We do not know for sure who the recipients were.
- John addressed a "chosen lady."
  - ~ Many commentators believe that the "chosen lady" was the church and that John used coded language to protect those receiving the letter.
    - * Persecution was harsh for believers.

> **NOTE:** Many missionaries today who are in countries that are closed to the Word of God, or closed to missionaries, speak in "coded" language. They substitute certain words for other words, so that they can speak about Jesus Christ.

  - ~ But this letter could also be written to a certain woman who John did not identify.

- Again, commentators will differ on the recipients of this letter. It was either:
  - ~ A woman and her children
  - ~ The church and the church members
- The one thing we do know: John knew these people and he loved them.

SECOND JOHN
Theme: Shun False Teachers

- Do not overlook how John referred to himself: "the elder."
  - ~ He was, indeed, elderly at the writing of this letter—possibly the oldest apostle that was living and chief "elder" in the church.
  - ~ An "elder" in the house of Israel was someone to be respected, even more so given John's position as an apostle.
  - ~ As such, John wanted these people to have the truth.

- The word "truth" is used five times in the first four verses.
- ✞ **2 John 1** "The elder to the chosen lady and her children, whom I love in **truth**; and not only I, but also all who know the **truth** …"
  - ~ The first two uses of "truth" involve a commendation for those who were demonstrating a godly walk in the faith, in truth.

> **NOTE:** Many people today express that they want to "know the truth" or that they are "looking for the truth everywhere." They don't find it because the truth to them is "what they want to hear."
> - In our culture today, truth has become subjective with the added possibility of being ever-changing.
> - But the word "true" is defined as that which is *"factual, accurate, correct, exact, real, and spot-on."*
> - ⇨ **Something that is "exact" or "spot-on" cannot be *sort of* "exact."**

****

- ❈ <u>**ILLUSTRATION:**</u> As Jesus stood before Pilate, just before He was crucified, it was clear that Pilate knew very little about Him but believed Him to be an innocent man. Pilate asked Jesus, "What is truth?" (Very much like the world today asks.) This encounter between Pilate and Jesus was striking. Why? The TRUTH was standing right before Pilate. This scene gives credence to the phrase "I wouldn't know the truth if it was standing right in front of me."

  Jesus had clearly stated that He was "the truth, the way, and the life." (John 14:6)

****

- When we speak of truth in regards to the New Testament teaching, what is truth?
  - ~ It is the gospel, the true facts regarding the Lord Jesus Christ.
    - * The virgin birth of Jesus Christ.
    - * The incarnation of Jesus Christ—He was fully God and fully man.
    - * The Divine Son of God.
    - * The sinless life of Jesus Christ.

* Crucified on a cross for the sins of the world.
* Died and was buried.
* Rose on the third day to live forevermore.
* He will return.

⇨ **These are the gospel truths that are "non-negotiable."**

> **NOTE:** Some beliefs or traditions may separate us into different denominations, but differences are ones that we can agree to disagree on. However, the "gospel truths" cannot be disputed or altered.

B. John understood that abiding truth is <u>ETERNAL</u>.

* In verse two, John uses the word "truth" again:

✝ **2 John 2** "… for the sake of the **truth** which abides in us and will be with us forever …"

* Truth abides in a believer and this abiding truth is eternal.
* This is an important point to understand:
  ~ Jesus Christ is the truth.
  ~ If a person is a believer, Jesus Christ abides in him through the Holy Spirit.
  ~ A believer has this truth forever—a believer cannot lose it—because it is all about Jesus and who He is, the Truth!

C. It pleased John to learn that some children were living in <u>OBEDIENCE</u>.

* John uses the word "truth" for the fourth time in verse four:

✝ **2 John 4** "I was very glad to find some of your children walking in **truth**, just as we have received commandment to do from the Father."

* There are different understandings as to what John meant by the phrase "some of your children."
  ~ If John was writing an individual woman, then he was expressing how pleased he was that some of her children had chosen to follow Jesus Christ.
  ~ If John was using "coded" language (suggested as a possibility) and writing to the church, then commentators believe it is possible John was acknowledging that some church members had left the church and joined the deceivers.

* "Walking in truth" means "allowing God's Word to control every area of your life."

~ Shouldn't this be the prayer of every parent and grandparent? That their children would know God's Word and walk in it—give their hearts to Christ early in their lives and never deviate from the truth?

> ❖ **APPLICATION:** There may be those in the class whose children are not walking in the truth and have become discouraged.
> - ~ Perhaps they have pre-teens or teenagers or college kids who are away at school.
> - ~ Many who now walk closely with the Lord as adults will comment on how they got into a group away from home and strayed from the truth they had been taught as children in their home churches.
>
> ⇨ **How do we combat such straying from the truth? Pray, pray, pray.**

- It is much easier to study the truth or argue about the truth than it is to actually practice the truth.
  - ~ We learned this in the book of James when he exhorted believers to be "doers of the Word, not merely hearers."
- John was making the same case as he urged the recipients to live out truth in obedience to God's Word.

⇨ **Knowing truth is not enough—believers must show the truth through obedience.**

II. JOHN COMMANDED HIS RECIPIENTS TO LOVE ONE ANOTHER (2 JOHN 5–6)

A. John's letter was a reminder to live out the <u>COMMANDMENTS</u> to love.

✝ **2 John 5** "Now I ask you, lady, not as though I were writing to you a new commandment, but the one which we have had from the beginning, that we love one another."

- He stated this was nothing new. The recipients had heard this command before.
- But John believed it was important to reiterate it.

- Jesus gave the criteria for a disciple of Christ:

✝ **John 13:35** "By this all men will know that you are My disciples, if you have love for one another."

> ★ **TEACHING TIP:**
>
> *Through the power of the Holy Spirit, believers can love—really love—others that they don't particularly "like."*

- Christian love is an act of the will. It is different from an emotional kind of love.
  - ~ It treats others as God treats people.
  - ~ It treats enemies—those who oppose you–with love.

SECOND JOHN
Theme: Shun False Teachers

- In this letter, John reminded them of the "love lessons" that Jesus had preached in the Sermon on the Mount.

✝ **Matthew 5:44** "But I say to you, love your enemies and pray for those who persecute you …"

- In each and every opportunity that presents itself, a believer is to do "good" toward others (friend or foe) because that is how Jesus would have responded.

B. John defined love as <u>OBEDIENCE</u> to Christ's commandments.

- Again John used Jesus' own words to define "true" love:

✝ **John 14:15** "If you love Me, you will keep My commandments."

✝ **John 13:34** "A new commandment I give to you, that you love one another, even as I have loved you, that you also love one another."

- John reiterated what he had said in 1 John:

✝ **1 John 3:23–24** "This is His commandment, that we believe in the name of His Son Jesus Christ, and love one another, just as He commanded us. The one who keeps His commandments abides in Him, and He in him. We know by this that He abides in us, by the Spirit whom He has given us."

⇨ **John's point was clear—it is impossible to love God and not love others.**

- John used three very important words: truth, love, and obedience.
  - ~ When we believe and accept truth, Christ, and the Word of God, we are saved *from* eternal judgment and are saved *to* a new life in Christ.
  - ~ Evidence of salvation is our obedience to His Word and our love for others.

III. JOHN CAUTIONED HIS RECIPIENTS TO WATCH OUT FOR FALSE TEACHERS (2 JOHN 7–13)

A. John warned about deceivers who denied Jesus' <u>COMING</u>.

✝ **2 John 7** "For many deceivers have gone out into the world, those who do not acknowledge Jesus Christ as coming in the flesh. This is the deceiver and the antichrist."

- They did not deny that Jesus had ever lived.
- They denied that He was the Messiah and the Son of God.
- They taught that Jesus was:
  - ~ Just another man, a human being.

SECOND JOHN
Theme: Shun False Teachers

     ~ Just a carpenter.

     ~ Just the son of Mary and Joseph.

- They denied the divinity of Jesus Christ when they claimed He was "just like" everybody else.
- They did describe Him as being a good teacher—we hear such comments today.

⇨ **False teachers would not say (and still will not say) that Jesus is the Son of God.**

- John called these false teachers "the deceiver" and the "antichrist."
- "Antichrist" means "against Christ."
- The sad reality is that people love a lie. They are willing to believe a lie, even when the truth makes far more sense.
- Human nature would rather believe lies and resist God's truth.

> ★ **TEACHING TIP:**
> *"A lie can travel halfway around the world while the truth is still putting on its shoes."*
> *~ Mark Twain*

⇨ **The lesson: the test of a true teacher is what he or she believes about Jesus Christ.**

     ~ Not simply *"if"* they believe in Him, but *"what"* they believe about Him.

     ~ If they are false teachers, the air will become chilly and a defensive posture will probably be taken.

     ~ If they are true teachers, their love for Jesus and who He is and what He has done for them will overflow into their conversation.

⇨ **False teachers can "profess" to know Jesus, but they do not "possess" Him in their hearts.**

B. John cautioned his recipients to not lose what has been <u>GAINED</u>.

✝ **2 John 8** "Watch yourselves, that you do not lose what we have accomplished, but that you may receive a full reward."

- Guard against regressing instead of progressing!
- False teachers will tell you they have something to give you but, in actuality, they do not have anything to give. Instead, they take away from what a believer already has.
- John was not discussing salvation here. He was speaking to the rewards of a believer.

C. John stated that Christian teaching must include <u>CHRIST</u> or the teacher is without God.

SECOND JOHN
Theme: Shun False Teachers

✝ **2 John 9** "Anyone who goes too far and does not abide in the teaching of Christ, does not have God; the one who abides in the teaching, he has both the Father and the Son."

- To compromise with false teaching was and is a danger.
  - ~ We can compromise just by keeping silent when we hear others speak untruth and we do not speak up— we know better, but we allow the "false" conversation to go on.
  - ~ False teachers can be very clever in their presentations—sometimes very argumentative or intimidating, while at other times very charismatic in their personality and selection of "Christian words" (sounds right but isn't).

> ★ **TEACHING TIP:**
> *Departure from the gospel is, in effect, a departure from God. The gospel message points people to a relationship with God.*

⇨ **Satan does not care what language is used—he doesn't care if we talk about Scripture or even quote it, just as long as we "misquote" it or add things that are not true.**

- John exhorted these believers to "abide" in the teachings of Christ.
- To "abide" is to be "rooted" or "grounded" in the Word of God—as believers, we must know His Word to discern the message of those trying to "uproot" us!

❖ **APPLICATION:** Have you had people knock on your door, often a pair, who want to discuss spiritual things? One may have a Bible opened and appear to be looking for a Scripture—while the other one has you engaged in an argument or debate.
  - ~ At first, they seem very nice but they become quite intimidating with their two on one approach.
  - ~ They speak quickly and use words that "sound" legitimate, but they are false.
  - ~ They may ask you to take their material—if you do, they believe you have given them a victory.
  - ~ They may have an "extra" book to give that they say is "additional" truth— suggesting that it will make your Bible "whole."

  ⇨ **The Holy Bible IS the whole truth—there is nothing to add to it.**

D. John commanded that those who come with false teaching must neither be RECEIVED or GREETED.

✝ **2 John 10** "If anyone comes to you and does not bring this teaching, do not receive him into your house, and do not give him a greeting ..."

SECOND JOHN
Theme: Shun False Teachers

- In John's day, there were itinerant teachers. Offering hospitality was a very important element of the culture.
- Families would open their homes to these teachers.
  - ~ This was a godsend for the teachers because the inns of that day were unsafe—often used for prostitution and having a clientele of murderers and thieves.
- Their heart for hospitality posed a problem—they began to entertain false teachers as well in their homes.
- So John instructed them:
  - ~ Do not acknowledge them with a greeting.
  - ~ Do nothing that could be construed as an endorsement or encouragement of their teaching.

> ★ **TEACHING TIP:**
> *In that day, many greeted one another with the phrase, "God speed."*
> *This was not a greeting that should be given to one opposing and denying Christ in their teaching.*

⇨ **Do not be fooled—a false teacher's goal is to undermine the true doctrine of Jesus Christ.**

- Christians are encouraged to open their homes to others, especially missionaries, preachers, and Bible teachers because they are called "fellow helpers in the faith" in Scripture. But this does not apply to those who "oppose" faith in Jesus Christ.

E. John further stated that if a false teacher was offered hospitality, the host would be GUILTY of participating in evil.

✞ **2 John 11** "… for the one who gives him a greeting participates in his evil deeds."

- By offering hospitality to a false teacher, a believer gave tacit approval to his evil.
- John was being firm—believers could not associate with anyone aligned as a deceiver and the antichrist.
- Christians must use discernment.
  - ~ If a teacher comes that does not agree with the true doctrine of Christ and teaches a false doctrine, then believers should not allow them inside their homes.

REVIEW:

⌑ Why was John so adamant about this?
1. Welcoming false teachers insinuated that heresy was just fine, acceptable.
2. Welcoming false teachers presented them a platform to influence others—by association and friendship.

SECOND JOHN
Theme: Shun False Teachers

3. Welcoming false teachers could be used as a "recommendation."
   - ~ In other words, they could go down the street and say, "I just stayed at ____ house."
   - ~ The person hearing this could think, "Well, I know they are strong believers, so this person (false teacher) must be okay."

⌑ John was NOT saying that believers can only host believers in their homes—our homes should be used to bring people to know the Lord, whether neighbors or friends, through warm hospitality.

⌑ John addressed not giving hospitality to anyone who campaigned against the foundations of Christian faith.

> **NOTE:** Tradition gives an example of how strongly John felt about this.
> - ♦ He was at a public bath when he saw a man, Cerinthus, who spoke heresy, enter.
> - ♦ John knew that Cerinthus was the head of a heretical sect in the town.
>   - ~ He taught that Jesus was just a man, the son of Joseph and Mary, and no more.
> - ♦ John jumped up and ran from the building—fearing he would be killed when the building collapsed under the righteous judgment of God!

F. John ended with the hope of personally <u>DELIVERING</u> the next message.

- ▪ It would seem that John had more to say, but not enough papyrus to write it out.

FINAL THOUGHTS AND APPLICATION

⌑ Second John is a tiny letter with a huge message.

⌑ Believers must be careful, alert, and discerning about who they entertain as teachers of the Word.

⌑ Believers should never let their guard down—there are imposters, counterfeiters, everywhere and they are good at making the "false" sound "true."

⌑ False teachers take what is real or true and "enhance" it by either adding error or subtracting truth.

⌑ Do not forget the warnings that have been given to us:
- ~ The false are "wolves in sheep's clothing."
- ~ Satan disguises himself as "an angel of light."
- ~ Satan is a roaring lion seeking to devour us.

SECOND JOHN
Theme: Shun False Teachers

⌑ As we began, people can easily be fooled by the false. Artificial flowers, make-up, and physical enhancements have all become an "art."

⌑ But more sinister and lethal is the reality of people being fooled by false doctrine regarding Jesus Christ—it happened in John's day and it happens today.

⇨ **Believers protect the truth when they prohibit the presence of untruth.**

❖ **<u>FINAL APPLICATION:</u> Today, just as in John's day, we must know the truth, show the truth, and refuse to fellowship with untruth in order to live in purity in our homes and churches.**

SECOND JOHN REVIEW HELPS

✧ **With Bibles closed and working in small groups, put all the New Testament books in order and give the theme, purpose, and author of each book.**

THIRD JOHN

Show Hospitality

You will do well to send them on their way
in a manner worthy of God.

3 John 6

SESSION SIXTY-FOUR: THIRD JOHN
Show Hospitality

✝ **Memory verse:** *"You will do well to send them on their way in a manner worthy of God."* *(3 John 6)*

Introduction: In this very personal letter, the apostle John focused on the practice of hospitality: that which shows the love of God to others. He applauded the gracious hospitality of Gaius, but also condemned the selfishness of Diotrephes "who loves to be the first among them".

- **Oral Review:** Please refer to the **REVIEW Section** in the following Teaching Guide Outline.

- **Homework:** Review the homework from the book of 2 John.

    Question on page 154
    Questions on pages 156–157
    Last question on page 160
    Questions on pages 161–163

- **Review Helps:** Written review is provided at the end of the teacher presentation. (Optional and time permitting.)

- **Teacher Presentation on the Book of Third John**

- **Learning for Life:** You may choose to discuss all or just one or two of the questions on page 175.

- **Closing prayer:** Pray that students could see God's heart toward hospitality. Believers should be hospitable and open their homes to others. Pray that, this week, each one of them would practice hospitality by inviting another family or friend in to share a meal with them in their home.

THIRD JOHN
Theme: Show Hospitality

<u>OUTLINE AID FOR TEACHERS:</u>

I. **THE INTRODUCTION (3 JOHN 1)**

   A. The witness of <u>GOD</u> proves the Word is true.

      1. It is divinely <u>INSPIRED</u>.

      2. It is <u>INERRANT</u>.

   B. The witness of <u>JESUS</u> proves the Word is true.

      1. Jesus is called the <u>WORD</u> and the Truth.

      2. Jesus quoted <u>SCRIPTURE</u> with authority and confidence.

II. **JOHN COMMENED GAIUS (3 JOHN 2–8)**

   A. John used the <u>GODLINESS</u> of Gaius as an example to all.

      1. He had <u>FAITHFULNESS</u> to the truth.

      2. He was <u>WALKING</u> in the truth.

   B. John encouraged the <u>GENEROSITY</u> of Gaius to continue.

      1. He was faithful in <u>DOING GOOD</u> for brothers of truth.

      2. He showed <u>HOSPITALITY</u> while working for the truth.

III. **JOHN CONDEMNED DIOTREPHES (3 JOHN 9–12)**

   A. John confronted the <u>PRIDE</u> of Diotrephes.

      1. He loved to be <u>FIRST</u>.

      2. He was <u>GOSSIPING</u> about John and the other teachers of truth.

      3. He refused <u>HOSPITALITY</u> to the brothers of truth.

      4. He put those faithful to the truth <u>OUT OF</u> the church.

B. John had <u>PRAISE</u> for Demetrius.

    1. He was in need of <u>HOSPITALITY</u>.

    2. He was spoken <u>WELL OF</u> by everyone.

IV. THE BENEDICTION (3 JOHN 13–15)

3 John

[Show Hospitality]

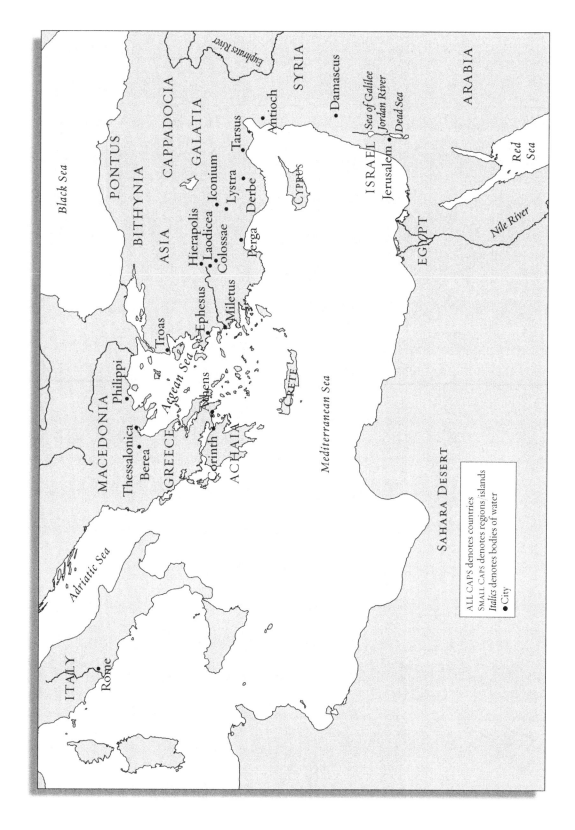

THIRD JOHN
Theme: Show Hospitality

THE BASICS:
⇨ **Who: The Author:** John
⇨ **What:** Encouraging fellowship with Christian brothers
⇨ **When:** Written around A.D. 90
⇨ **Where:** Written from Ephesus to the churches in Asia
⇨ **Why:** To commend Gaius on his walk of truth and hospitality to the missionaries and to recommend Demetrius while rebuking Diotrephes for his pride and rebellion

MEMORY VERSE: *"You will do well to send them on their way in a manner worthy of God."*
3 John 6

****

REVIEW:

⌘ The *Old Testament History* books addressed sin, judgment, and death (the consequences of sin), and the promised Messiah.

⌘ The *New Testament History* books addressed Jesus' first coming, His time on earth, and the birth of the church.

⌘ In *Paul's Letters to the Churches*, Paul addressed the following:
  ~ **Romans:** God's righteousness described.
  ~ **First Corinthians:** Church's problems corrected.
  ~ **Second Corinthians:** Paul's ministry defended.
  ~ **Galatians:** Believers' freedom in Christ.
  ~ **Ephesians:** Believers' holy walk.
  ~ **Philippians:** Believers' joy in Christ.
  ~ **Colossians:** Believers' completion in Christ.
  ~ **First Thessalonians:** The return of the Lord.
  ~ **Second Thessalonians:** The Day of the Lord.

⌘ In *Paul's Letters to Pastors*, Paul addressed the following:
  ~ **First Timothy:** Instructions on leadership.
  ~ **Second Timothy:** Instructions on endurance.
  ~ **Titus:** Instructions on church order.
  ~ **Philemon:** Instructions on forgiveness.

⌘ In *Other Letters and Revelation*, the authors addressed:
  ~ **Hebrews:** The superiority of Jesus Christ. The author encouraged the Jewish believers who were suffering for their faith to endure—not to turn back to Judaism. Nothing could compare to what they had in Christ.

THIRD JOHN
Theme: Show Hospitality

- ~ **James:** True faith—it will have works to prove it.
- ~ **First Peter:** Suffering steadfastly—manifesting holiness, harmony, and humility in times of crisis. Focus on suffering coming from outside the church.
- ~ **Second Peter:** Identify false teachers.
- ~ **First John:** Fellowship with God.
- ~ **Second John:** Shunning false teachers—encouraging believers to protect the truth by prohibiting the presence of untruth in their lives.

OVERVIEW:

- Hospitality can be tricky as seen in the following story.

****

❊ **ILLUSTRATION:** A story was told about an English teacher who planned to take a sabbatical in Switzerland. She visited the town in which she planned on staying and enlisted the help of a schoolmaster to help her find a place to stay. She found a room and signed the necessary contract to move in.

As she returned to England to gather her belongings, it occurred to her that she had not seen a bathroom or a "water closet," as she called it, where she would be staying. She wrote a letter to the schoolmaster and asked him if the "WC" ("water closet") was either in or near her apartment. Upon receiving the letter, the schoolmaster was taken aback because he had never heard of a "WC." He took the letter to the parish priest for help in understanding the English woman's question. The two decided that she must have been referring to the Wayside Chapel, which was nearby. This was the answer she received a couple of days later.

Dear Madam – the WC is located nine miles from the house. It is located in the heart of a beautiful grove of trees. It will seat 150 people at one time. It is open on Tuesdays, Thursdays, and Sundays. It might interest you to know that my daughter met her husband at the WC. I will close now with the desire to accommodate you in every possible way and will be happy to save you a seat either down in front or by the door, as you prefer.

****

⇨ **The purpose of John's letter was to address the subject of hospitality by comparing two approaches: the true way, out of love for the brethren, and the proud way, out of arrogance.**

- Third John was also written by the apostle John.
- Commentators are not exactly sure when he wrote this letter and from where, but most agree that it was written between 85 and 95 A.D. from Ephesus.

THIRD JOHN
Theme: Show Hospitality

- There is also no certainty as to which church he was writing, but it would seem it was located in the general area of Asia.
- The recipient of the letter was John's dear friend, Gaius, who he loved, admired, and considered warm-hearted.
- John was known for giving special permission to teachers and evangelists to go on missionary journeys.
  - ~ In his sending out of these missionaries, he expected believers to welcome them in "His name"— welcome them in the name of Jesus Christ.
- John's friend, Demetrius, seemed to be one of the teachers that he had sent out to the churches in Asia (where Gaius is), but Demetrius was sent away and was not received!
  - * He apparently reported this experience to John who had now sent Demetrius back with this letter.

- Third John is only fifteen verses long, but you will see that it is full of information.
- The letter is typical of John's writing—focusing on truth, love, and joy.
- It is also filled with comparisons and contrasts.
  - ~ Being hospitable and being inhospitable
  - ~ Being selfless and being selfish
  - ~ Being humble and being arrogant

- In this letter, John spoke to a subject dear to his heart—hospitality.
  - ~ In 1 John, he addressed fellowship with God.
  - ~ In 2 John, he exhorted them not to have fellowship with false teachers.
  - ~ In 3 John, he spoke to having fellowship with brothers and sisters in Christ.

- He began the letter addressing what is most precious to John's heart: truth.
  - ~ "Truth" is mentioned six different times and will be compared to lies.

- When we studied the book of Philemon, we learned that the Word of God is truth. We looked at external reasons that we can believe this:
  1. It has been witnessed in history.
  2. It has been witnessed in prophecy.
  3. It has been witnessed by the ability to survive (we are still studying it today).

NOTE: Before we dive into 3 John, we will look at how God the Father and Jesus testify that the Word of God is truth.

I.   THE INTRODUCTION (3 JOHN 1)

A. The witness of <u>GOD</u> proves the Word is true.

1. It is divinely <u>INSPIRED</u>.

- God Himself says that this is His Word:

✠ **2 Timothy 3:16** "All Scripture is inspired by God and profitable for teaching, for reproof, for correction, for training in righteousness;"

✠ **2 Peter 1:20–21** "But know this first of all, that no prophecy of Scripture is a matter of one's own interpretation, for no prophecy was ever made by an act of human will, but men moved by the Holy Spirit spoke from God."

- God said that He used ordinary men to speak His word by infusing them with His extraordinary spirit, the Holy Spirit.

2. It is <u>INERRANT</u>.

- To be "inerrant" is to be "without error."
- This is based on the very character of God:
  - ~ God is perfect.
  - ~ God cannot lie.
  - ~ God is holy.
  - ~ God is pure.
  - ~ God is righteous.
- Jesus Himself testified that the Word is truth:

✠ **John 17:17** "Sanctify them in the truth; Your word is truth."

B. The witness of <u>JESUS</u> proves the Word is true.

1. Jesus is called the <u>WORD</u> and the truth.

✠ **John 1:1** "In the beginning was the Word, and the Word was with God, and the Word was God."

✠ **John 14:6** "Jesus said to him, 'I am the way, and the truth, and the life ...'"

- Jesus is the Word incarnate—He is the truth.

2. Jesus quoted <u>SCRIPTURE</u> with authority and confidence.

- When Jesus was tempted in the desert, how did He respond to the evil one, Satan?
  - ~ With Scripture—only the Word.
  - ~ He did not apologize for the Word.
  - ~ He did not try to change the Word.
  - ~ Jesus only quoted Scripture.

> ★ **TEACHING TIP:**
>
> *Why did Jesus not amend or change the Word? Because it is true! His very witness to it proves the Word of God is truth.*

- When He was confronted by the Jews, Jesus reminded them that Scripture could not be broken. He, in fact, came to fulfill it. (John 10:35)
  - ~ Jesus did not amend the Word—He did not change it.
- Jesus quoted and validated the authority of the Word.
  - ~ He quoted things from the prophets and fulfilled the prophecy of the prophets.

- John knew this because He saw Jesus live out His confidence in the Word of God.
- So, in this letter, John spoke to:
  - ~ The truth being uplifted.
  - ~ Walking in the truth.
  - ~ Knowing the truth.
  - ~ Speaking the truth.
- To John, the truth—the Word of God—was a precious treasure to be lived out and protected because it was from God

II. JOHN COMMENDED GAIUS (3 JOHN 2–8)

A. John used the <u>GODLINESS</u> of Gaius as an example to all.

✞ **3 John 2–3** "Beloved, I pray that in all respects you may prosper and be in good health, just as your soul prospers. For I was very glad when brethren came and testified to your truth, that is, how you are walking in truth."

- John referred to Gaius as "beloved"—he uses this endearing term four times when referring to Gaius in this letter. (3 John 1–2, 5, 11)
- John prayed that his material prosperity and good health would thrive, as his soul did.

> **NOTE:** Why would John address Gaius' physical health? Simply put: the Gnostics.
> - The Gnostics followed Peter, Paul, and John with a goal to undermine their authority and teaching.
> - The Gnostics believed that all matter was evil (including the body)—only the spirit was good.
> - John prayed that Gaius' physical body was in good health—he demonstrated his

1. He had <u>FAITHFULNESS</u> to the truth.

- John had a heartfelt appreciation for Gaius' faithfulness to the truth.
- He prayed that Gaius would continue to be faithful.
- Gaius was under attack in this small church.
  - ~ His stance on truth was under attack from other church members.

THIRD JOHN
Theme: Show Hospitality

- John understood such pressure and wanted to encourage Gaius that his faithfulness to the truth was known by other brothers of faith, not John alone.

    ### 2. He was **WALKING** in the truth.

✝ **3 John 4** "I have no greater joy than this, to hear of my children walking in the truth."

- "Walking in the truth" involves living according to the Word of God, adhering to it steadfastly as a way of life—walking IN the good news of Jesus Christ.
- What is the opposite of truth? Lies. Who is the father of lies? Satan.
    ~ There were lies being touted in this church.
    ~ Gaius was directly confronting these lies.

- Jesus spoke directly to the character of Satan:

✝ **John 8:44** "You are of your father the devil, and you want to do the desires of your father. He was a murderer from the beginning, and does not stand in the truth because there is no truth in him. Whenever he speaks a lie, he speaks from his own nature, for he is a liar and the father of lies."

****

❋ **ILLUSTRATION:** A woman shared that, before she became a Christian, she walked in the ways of the world. She confessed that she was a liar—not just "white lies" but big lies. Her attitude was that everyone lied, so why shouldn't she as well?

Then she came to Jesus. She realized she had become a child of God and, in that relationship, she represented Him. She knew that Jesus Christ was truth, so as God's daughter she needed to be a child of truth—walk in truth, speak in truth, live in truth.

However, the change did not come overnight. In fact, she shared, "I found myself unable to get away with a lie. No matter what it was—my lie was discovered and I had to confess it. Finally, I just planted myself in God's Word. These are a few things that the Lord showed me:

1. *Keep your tongue from evil and your lips from speaking deceit. (Psalm 34:13)*
2. *The acquisition of treasures by a lying tongue Is a fleeting vapor, the pursuit of death. (Proverbs 21:6)*
3. *A false witness will not go unpunished, And he who tells lies will not escape. (Proverbs 19:5)*
4. *Lying lips are an abomination to the Lord, But those who deal faithfully are His delight. (Proverbs 12:22)*

"I no longer wanted to be a woman of the world—I wanted to be a woman of the Word. Things changed in our family. Lying became 'non-negotiable' in our home. Lies were

THIRD JOHN
Theme: Show Hospitality

dealt with swiftly and harshly. Why? Because I wanted to be able to say, 'I have no greater joy than to know my children are walking in the truth.' Not because they were representing me, but because they were representing the God of truth, Jesus."

****

- Gaius was a delight to John because he applied God's truth to his daily walk!

B. John encouraged the <u>GENEROSITY</u> of Gaius to continue.

1. He was faithful in <u>DOING GOOD</u> for brothers of truth.

2. He showed <u>HOSPITALITY</u> while working for the truth.

<u>3 John 5–8</u>
- Gaius provided a home (lodging) for the teachers, preachers, and evangelists as they traveled from community to community.
- John had insisted that believers receive their brothers of Truth—Gaius responded by throwing his doors wide open!
- As you may recall in our last study, it was not safe for these traveling teachers, preachers, and evangelists to stay in the local inns—most were dangerous and immoral.
- John had a secondary reason that he did not want these brothers to stay in the inns or in homes of unbelievers:
  - ~ He did not want to put unbelievers out.
  - ~ He did not want them to question the motives of these Christians.

- John thought believers should receive believers—it was a manner in which one could serve Jesus.

> ❖ **APPLICATION:** The truth is, hospitality is a hard thing to do—and in our present day, it is basically a lost art.
>   - ~ People hardly ever sit down to dinner with their own families, let alone inviting others over.
>   - ~ Opening one's door, as Gaius did, can be inconvenient and expensive:
>   - ⋆ More laundry
>   - ⋆ More mouths to feed
>   - ⋆ Less privacy
>   - ⋆ More to do with less time to do it
>
> ⇨ **Believers today have forgotten that hospitality, in God's economy, demonstrates our love for Christ and His people.**

THIRD JOHN
Theme: Show Hospitality

⇨ **Gaius is an example of how simple hospitality reflects love for God's Word and truth.**

- John moved from the subject of truth and love to the arena of pride and strife.

III. JOHN CONDEMNED DIOTREPHES (3 JOHN 9–12)

A. John confronted the <u>PRIDE</u> of Diotrephes.

1. He loved to be <u>FIRST</u>.

✝ **3 John 9** "I wrote something to the church; but Diotrephes, who loves to be first among them, does not accept what we say."

> ★ **TEACHING TIP:**
>
> *A true servant, a true leader, is humble and subjects himself to authority. It is interesting to note that the one who refuses to be submissive can become the greatest tyrant.*

- Diotrephes' attitude was diametrically opposed to how Gaius thought and acted.
- Whereas Gaius submitted to the authority of John, Diotrephes did not.
- Diotrephes' pride was causing the church to split.

⇨ **It is an essential violation of love to put oneself first.**
  - ~ The first shall be last and the last shall be first in the ways of truth, in the ways of the Word.

- Pride had taken over Diotrephes' life and pride had taken over the church.

- The great missionary, Hudson Taylor, said, "All God's giants have been weak men who did great things for God because they reckoned on God being with them."
  - ~ God is not limited by a man's limitations.
  - ~ It brings God greater glory when a man recognizes this truism.

- Diotrephes did not think or act in a posture of submission.
- He put himself above the apostles.
- His disobedience manifested his lack of love for his fellow believers and he was not willing to change.

2. He was <u>GOSSIPING</u> about John and the other teachers of truth.

✝ **3 John 10a** "For this reason, if I come, I will call attention to his deeds which he does, unjustly accusing us with wicked words;"

- Gossip is wicked words—it lies.

- Diotrephes was lying about John and believers that were coming to the church, the traveling missionaries.
- As stated before, a lie is the opposite of truth—and we, as believers, know the origins of such lies.
  - ~ Diotrephes was not following the Word of truth.
  - ~ He was following the prince of this world.

3. He refused <u>HOSPITALITY</u> to the brothers of truth.

✝ **3 John 10b** "… and not satisfied with this, he himself does not receive the brethren, either …"

4. He put those faithful to the truth <u>OUT OF</u> the church.

✝ **3 John 10c** "… and he forbids those who desire to do so and puts them out of the church."

- As a prideful man, it was his way or the proverbial "highway."
- Diotrephes had placed himself in the position of deciding who was allowed in the church and who was not.

- It appears that Demetrius, the one who brought this letter, had been a victim of this "turning away"—he had not been received by Diotrephes.

- John turned his attention to the letter carrier.

> ✴ **TEACHING TIP:**
> *Could it be that John had hoped to give Diotrephes an opportunity to repent and ask forgiveness for his inhospitable and unloving ways by having Demetrius as the letter carrier?*

B. John had <u>PRAISE</u> for Demetrius.

1. He was in need of <u>HOSPITALITY</u>.

2. He was spoken <u>WELL OF</u> by everyone.

- John must have given Demetrius a full commission to not only represent him and the other apostles, but also Jesus Christ.
- He had a great reference pool—everyone!

> ✴ **TEACHING TIP:**
> *Wouldn't you love to have this said of you, of your testimony to the Lord, because of how you lived?*

✝ **3 John 12** "Demetrius has received a good testimony from everyone, and from the truth itself; and we add our testimony, and you know that our testimony is true."
  - ~ He had received a good testimony from people AND from the truth itself.

~ John personified "truth" and basically said, "If truth was a person, he would rave about Demetrius. He would have written him a recommendation."

IV. THE BENEDICTION (3 JOHN 13–15)

✠ **3 John 13-15** "I had many things to write to you, but I am not willing to write them to you with pen and ink; but I hope to see you shortly, and we will speak face to face. Peace be to you. The friends greet you. Greet the friends by name."

- John hoped to come see these believers in person.
- By this time, he was a very old man.
- When he traveled with Jesus, he was the benefactor of people that were hospitable because we know that Jesus did not have "a place to lay His head."
- For the three years, he followed Jesus; he was probably a guest in peoples' homes.
- Now, living in Ephesus, he received people in the name of Jesus Christ, in the name of truth, as a giver and receiver of the Word.

FINAL THOUGHTS AND APPLICATION

¤ The application of this book is quite simple and clear:
   ~ You can be a "Gaius" and represent Jesus Christ practically by inviting people into your home in the name of the Word … in love and in truth … OR
   ~ You can be a Diotrephes, willing to undermine Christ's authority and misrepresent the Word … in arrogance and pride.

❖ **FINAL APPLICATION: Hospitality is a crucial and practical way to show Christ's love to the body.**

THIRD JOHN REVIEW HELPS

✧ **Have each student choose the book in the Bible that has meant the most to them and write out why they chose that book, what they have learned from it, and how it has impacted their life.**

JUDE

Contend for the Faith

Contend earnestly for the faith which was

once for all handed down to the saints.

Jude 3

SESSION SIXTY-FIVE: JUDE
Contend for the Faith

☩ **Memory verse:** *"…contend earnestly for the faith which was once for all handed down to the saints."* *(Jude 3)*

Introduction: Like James, Jude was the half-brother of Jesus. Here, in this short letter, he vehemently condemns the heretics and exhorts the believers to contend for the faith, "building yourselves up on your most holy faith, praying in the Holy Spirit, and keeping yourselves in the love of God".

- **Oral Review:** Please refer to the **REVIEW Section** in the following Teaching Guide Outline.

- **Homework:** Review the homework from the book of 3 John.

    Questions on pages 180–181
    Questions on page 183
    Second question on page 184
    Discuss the application on page 187 (second paragraph)

- **Review Helps:** Written review is provided at the end of the teacher presentation. (Optional and time permitting.)

- **Teacher Presentation on the Book of Jude**

- **Learning for Life:** You may choose to discuss all or just one or two of the questions on page 200.

- **Closing prayer:** Pray that students will submit to God's authority through His Word and will understand the power of Satan.

JUDE
Theme: Contend for the Faith

OUTLINE AID FOR TEACHERS:

I. **WARNING ABOUT FALSE TEACHERS: DANGER FOR THE BELIEVERS (JUDE1–4)**

A. False teachers had crept into the church unnoticed.

1. They rejected the Ruler by refusing to submit to God's <u>AUTHORITY</u>.

2. They lived licentiously by practicing <u>IMMORALITY</u> without shame.

3. They denied the Deity by denying with their words and lifestyle that Jesus is <u>GOD</u>.

II. **DESCRIPTION OF FALSE TEACHERS (JUDE 5–16)**

A. Jude gave three Old Testament descriptions of apostasy and God's judgment:

1. <u>ISRAEL</u> rejected the Ruler by not believing God and refusing to enter the Promised Land. All died except Joshua and Caleb.

2. <u>ANGELS</u> denied the Deity. Those who rebelled were bound for the Day of Judgment.

3. <u>SODOM</u> and Gomorrah lived licentiously. All were destroyed.

Lesson #1: God always judges rebellion. Judgment is coming!

B. God created angels as spirit beings to <u>WORSHIP</u> God and <u>MINISTER</u> to men.

1. Gabriel delivered <u>MESSAGES</u> to men.

2. Michael fought <u>BATTLES</u> for men.

3. Satan (serpent, Devil) rebelled and desires to <u>DECEIVE</u> men.

4. God gave two weapons to fight Satan: the <u>WORD</u> of God and the <u>NAME</u> of God.

Lesson #2: Satan must be fought with God's authority, not our own.

C. Jude gave three examples of the motives of apostates and the consequences.

1. The way of Cain—<u>SELF</u>-righteous religion of trusting own works. Cain departed from the presence of the Lord.

2. The error of Balaam—<u>GREED</u> or religion for material gain. Balaam was killed by the sword.

3. The rebellion of Korah—<u>RESISTING</u> the authority God has given another. Korah perished.

D. False teachers are dangerous, useless, fruitless, and doomed for <u>DESTRUCTION</u>.

III.   DEFENSE AGAINST FALSE TEACHERS: DUTY OF THE BELIEVERS (JUDE 17–23)

A. Contend for the faith by <u>REMEMBERING</u> the Word's warning about false teachers.

B. Build yourself up in the faith by <u>PRAYING</u> in the Holy Spirit.

C. Keep yourself in God's love by <u>OBEYING</u> (see John 15:10).

IV.   VICTORY OVER FALSE TEACHERS (JUDE 24–25)

A. Only Jesus is able to keep you from <u>STUMBLING</u>.

B. Jesus is <u>GOD</u> our Savior with glory, majesty, and authority.

Lesson #3: Jesus, who keeps the apostate for judgment, keeps us from falling.

JUDE
[Contend for the Faith]

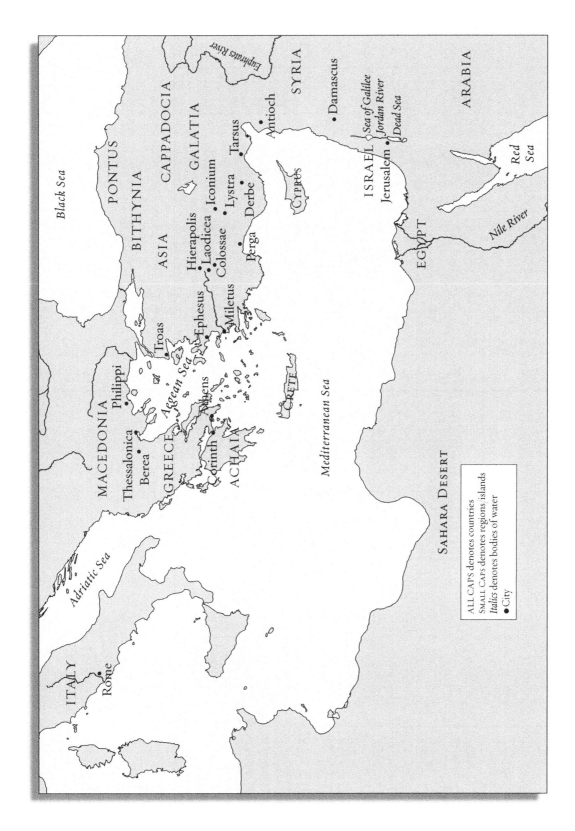

ALL CAPS denotes countries
SMALL CAPS denotes regions/islands
Italics denotes bodies of water
● City

JUDE

JUDE
Theme: Contend for the Faith

THE BASICS:
- ⇨ **Who: The Author:** Jude, brother of James and half-brother of Jesus
- ⇨ **What:** Encouragement of believers to contend for the faith
- ⇨ **When:** Written around A.D. 66–69
- ⇨ **Where:** Unknown
- ⇨ **Why:** False teachers had infiltrated the church

MEMORY VERSE: *"…contend earnestly for the faith which was once for all handed down to the saints." Jude 3*

****

REVIEW:

- ⌺ The *Old Testament History* books addressed sin, judgment, and death (the consequences of sin), and the promised Messiah.

- ⌺ The *New Testament History* books addressed Jesus' first coming, His time on earth, and the birth of the church.

- ⌺ In *Paul's Letters to the Churches*, Paul addressed the following:
  - ~ **Romans:** God's righteousness described.
  - ~ **First Corinthians:** Church's problems corrected.
  - ~ **Second Corinthians:** Paul's ministry defended.
  - ~ **Galatians:** Believers' freedom in Christ.
  - ~ **Ephesians:** Believers' holy walk.
  - ~ **Philippians:** Believers' joy in Christ.
  - ~ **Colossians:** Believers' completion in Christ.
  - ~ **First Thessalonians:** The return of the Lord.
  - ~ **Second Thessalonians:** The Day of the Lord.

- ⌺ In *Paul's Letters to Pastors*, Paul addressed the following:
  - ~ **First Timothy:** Instructions on leadership.
  - ~ **Second Timothy:** Instructions on endurance.
  - ~ **Titus:** Instructions on church order.
  - ~ **Philemon:** Instructions on forgiveness.

- ⌺ In *Other Letters and Revelation*, the authors addressed:
  - ~ **Hebrews:** Christ's superiority.
  - ~ **James:** Live faith through works.
  - ~ **First Peter:** Suffer steadfastly.
  - ~ **Second Peter:** Identify false teachers.

JUDE
Theme: Contend for the Faith

- ~ **First John:** Fellowship with God.
- ~ **Second John:** Shun false teachers.
- ~ **Third John:** Showing hospitality to fellow believers demonstrates God's truth and love.

OVERVIEW:

****

❋ **ILLUSTRATION:** A banker became aware that someone had stolen a check. The thief erased or washed off the name of the true account holder and the amount of the check, then rewrote the check to himself for one thousand dollars. This thief had pulled this scam at other banks, but now was attempting to cash a false check in the banker's institution. An alert cashier sounded the office alarm. The banker called the police, and then followed the man out of the bank. The thief was arrested. Why? Because someone sounded an alarm—someone was paying attention!

****

- God had been sounding an alarm throughout the New Testament.
  - ~ He has warned believers to be on the alert for false teachers. They wanted to steal something far more valuable than money—they wanted to steal a believer's faith!

- Jesus taught this on the Sermon on the Mount:
- ✝ **Matthew 7:15** "Beware of the false prophets, who come to you in sheep's clothing, but inwardly are ravenous wolves."

- Peter taught this in 2 Peter:
- ✝ **2 Peter 2:1** "But false prophets also arose among the people, just as there will also be false teachers among you, who will secretly introduce destructive heresies, even denying the Master who bought them ..."

- But God also spoke a message of warning through the prophets in the Old Testament: "Get right with God—judgment is coming!" (As an example, Jeremiah 2:35)
- In the New Testament, God seems to say, "Stay right with God! Ignore the false teachers because judgment is coming."

- The author of the book is Jude, the brother of James, who wrote the book of James.
  - ~ Given Jude's relationship with James, he was also the half-brother of Jesus.
  - ~ We know that the brothers of Jesus did not believe in Him until after His resurrection, but were in the Upper Room at the coming of the Holy Spirit. (Acts 1:13–14)

JUDE
Theme: Contend for the Faith

- Jude wrote to believers—those to whom he referred to in verse 2 as:
  - ~ Beloved in God the Father
  - ~ Kept for Jesus Christ

- Though we know Jude wrote believers, we are not certain who they were or where they lived.
- Jude's writing style was one of repetition—he stated his thoughts in "triplicates."
- The book of Jude is very similar to the book of 2 Peter—there is a debate about which letter was written first.
- It would seem that 2 Peter was written first because:
  1. Jude was written (A.D. 66–69) after Peter was martyred (A.D. 64–66).
  2. Jude quotes 2 Peter. (Jude 17–19)
  3. Peter warned about the false teachers coming, whereas Jude spoke in the past tense, stating that they had already come.

- The book of Jude is a called a "picture" of the last days.
- It is the perfect introduction to the book of Revelation because Jude explained why judgment was coming and why it was necessary—the judgment presented in Revelation.

⇨ **The purpose of the book of Jude was to encourage believers to contend for their faith in Jesus Christ.**

I. WARNING ABOUT FALSE TEACHERS: DANGER FOR THE BELIEVERS (JUDE 1–4)

- Jude stated up front his reason for writing:

✞ **Jude 3** "Beloved, while I was making every effort to write you about our common salvation, I felt the necessity to write to you appealing that you contend earnestly for the faith which was once for all handed down to the saints."

- ~ He had actually begun one letter addressing their common salvation, but felt compelled to change his focus to contending for the faith.

- "Contend" is an interesting word. It means "to struggle for" or "agonize over."
- The tense of the verb in this verse is one that expresses a continual action—in other words, a persistent, constant struggling for or agonizing over the faith.

> **★ TEACHING TIP:**
> *The word "contend" is the same word used for "wrestling." Wrestling is a sport that demands every ounce of the athlete's energy. It demands that the wrestler be in good shape for a hand-to-hand struggle.*

JUDE
Theme: Contend for the Faith

⇨ **Jude wanted the believers to understand that they needed to be in great spiritual shape to wrestle—to contend—for the faith.**

- Jude explained why they needed to be ready to defend the faith.

A. False teachers had crept into the church unnoticed.

✝ **Jude 4** "For certain persons have crept in unnoticed, those who were long beforehand marked out for this condemnation, ungodly persons who turn the grace of our God into licentiousness and deny our only Master and Lord, Jesus Christ."

1. They rejected the Ruler by refusing to submit to God's <u>AUTHORITY</u>.

- Jude referred to them as "ungodly" men—whatever they "pretended" to be, whether "religious" or "pious," it was a false charade.
- They "crept in" with their false teaching—leading others away from God.
- Why? God was not their god—they refused to surrender to His authority.

> ★ **TEACHING TIP:**
> *Do not miss the progression that Jude presented:*
> ***First:*** *they rejected God as their Ruler.*
> ***Second:*** *because they rejected the "Ruler," they could rationalize living decadently.*
> ***Third:*** *because they are living licentiously, they denied the deity of Jesus. To admit Jesus is God would cause them to stop living in a constant sinful lifestyle.*

2. They lived licentiously by practicing <u>IMMORALITY</u> without shame.

- Jude stated that these false teachers turned God's grace into a platform to rationalize a sinful lifestyle.
  - ~ They taught that believers were now "under grace," which somehow exempted them from obeying God's law, His Word.
  - ~ They taught that "grace" permitted them to live as they pleased—in other words, a license to sin.
- What compounded the perverse nature of their actions was their shamelessness in indulging their passions—they sinned in the "light of day" with seemingly no remorse.

3. They denied the Deity by denying with their words and lifestyle that Jesus is <u>GOD</u>.

- The idea here is that the doctrines that these false teachers held amounted to a denial of the only true God, the Savior—their actions gave witness to their unbelief.
- And because they denied the deity of Jesu Christ, they would be judged.

JUDE
Theme: Contend for the Faith

⇨ **Jude sets forth a clear progression: sin leads to judgment, rejecting God leads to judgment.**

> **NOTE:** The question must be asked: how could these false teachers have "crept in unnoticed?"
> - The only plausible answer—the church was asleep!

II. DESCRIPTION OF FALSE TEACHERS (JUDE 5–16)

A. Jude gave three Old Testament descriptions of apostasy and God's judgment:

<u>Jude 5–7</u>

1. **<u>ISRAEL</u> rejected the Ruler by not believing God and refusing to enter the Promised Land. All died except Joshua and Caleb.**

✟ **Jude 5** "Now I desire to remind you, though you know all things once for all, that the Lord, after saving a people out of the land of Egypt, subsequently destroyed those who did not believe."

- We know this story—God delivered the people of Israel from Egypt. He did it with miracles.
  - ~ God sent the plagues.
  - ~ He parted the Red Sea, and then released the water to drown the Egyptian army, who wanted to once more enslave the Israelites.
- Yet, when the Israelites reached the boundaries of the Promised Land, they refused to enter.
- Their refusal was a rejection of God, the Ruler, who had told them to enter the land.
- Not only did they reject entrance into the Promised Land, they decided that they wanted to go back to Egypt, to a life of slavery—back to bondage!
- God saw this as "unbelief" and destroyed the whole generation who had made this decision to reject the Promised Land—except for Joshua and Caleb who were the only ones who wanted to enter in and believed God could and would protect the people.

2. **<u>ANGELS</u> denied the Deity. Those who rebelled were bound for the Day of Judgment.**

✟ **Jude 6** "And angels who did not keep their own domain, but abandoned their proper abode, He has kept in eternal bonds under darkness for the judgment of the great day..."

JUDE
Theme: Contend for the Faith

3. <u>SODOM</u> and Gomorrah lived licentiously. All were destroyed.

✝ **Jude 7** "… just as Sodom and Gomorrah and the cities around them, since they in the same way as these indulged in gross immorality and went after strange flesh, are exhibited as an example in undergoing the punishment of eternal fire."

NOTE: There are two views about the phrase—"who did not keep their own domain, but abandoned their proper abode."

~ **First View**: It connects verses 6 and 7.
  * It suggests that the "these" in verse 7 refer to the angels in verse 6.
  * Therefore, angels and the people in Sodom and Gomorrah both went after strange flesh, indulging in gross immorality.
  * This view uses Genesis 6 and the book of Job to support it:
    1. Genesis 6: stated that the sons of God married the daughters of men, producing a race of giants.
    2. Job: refers to angels as "sons of God."
  * The conclusion: angels left their own abode and had sex with daughters of men producing a race of giants.

⇨ **Problem #1 with View One:**
  a. In Genesis, God went on to say that He was grieved in His heart that He had made man, that He would not continue to strive with men, that He would give them 75–100+ years and then send a flood to destroy them.
  b. If angels had done something so gross as having sex with humans, wouldn't God have said that He would not continue to strive with men *and* angels?

~ **Second View**: This view does not connect verse 6 with verse 7.
  a. Genesis 6: It states that the "sons of God" were godly people and the "daughters of men" were ungodly people who intermarried.
  b. It states that "these" in verse 7 refers to false teachers, just like those in Sodom and Gomorrah who indulged in gross immorality.

⇨ **In this view, the angels would be those in the original rebellion of Satan when he fell.**

■ It is important to notice the consequences that Jude laid out in these three scenarios:
  1. When Israel refused to obey God, the people died.
  2. When the angels refused to obey God, they were bound for judgment.
  3. In Sodom and Gomorrah, all were destroyed.

JUDE
Theme: Contend for the Faith

Lesson #1: God always judges rebellion. Judgment is coming!

✞ **Jude 8a** "Yet in the same way these men, also by dreaming, defile the flesh and reject authority …"

> ★ **TEACHING TIP:**
> *Do we tell our children something very important only once? No, we repeat ourselves—wanting the message to "sink in." This is what Jude did.*

- Jude repeated himself and once again spoke to how the people rejected God's authority and defiled their flesh.

- **Jude 8b–9**
- At the end of verse 8, Jude stated—"…and revile angelic majesties."
  - ~ He was speaking of the false teachers who reviled angelic majesties.
- In verse 9, Jude referenced a scene between the archangel and the devil:
  - ~ They disputed and argued over Moses' body.
  - ~ Michael, however, did not dare pronounce a judgment against Satan—instead, Michael said, "The Lord rebuke you!"
    - ⋆ To rebuke took more authority than Michael had been given, so he allowed God to do the rebuking of Satan.
- Jude was contrasting the prideful arrogance of the false teachers who spoke evil of God's angelic host.

B. God created angels as spirit beings to <u>WORSHIP</u> God and <u>MINISTER</u> to men.

- In the first nine verses of Jude, angels have been mentioned three times.
- Their role: To worship and serve God and to minister to men.
- Their number: The book of Revelation states that there are 10,000 times 10,000 and thousands of thousands. (Revelation 5:11)

- We will look at three angels: Gabriel, Michael, and Satan.

1. Gabriel delivered <u>MESSAGES</u> to men.

- He brought messages to the following:
  - ~ **Daniel:** regarding the visions he had. (Daniel 8:16, 9:21)
  - ~ **Zechariah:** regarding the birth of a son (John the Baptist) and the "muting" of Zechariah for unbelief regarding the news of an upcoming child. (Luke 1:11–20)
  - ~ **Mary:** regarding the birth of Jesus, the Messiah. (Luke 1:26–38)

2. Michael fought **BATTLES** for men.

- We just read about him in verses 8 and 9. But there are other references.
- In the book of Daniel, Michael fought a battle against the demonic power that tried to prevent him from giving God's words of understanding to Daniel. (Daniel 10:10–14)

  - In the book of Revelation, we learn more about Michael:

✞ **Revelation 12:7** "And there was war in heaven, Michael and his angels waging war with the dragon."

  ~ Michael has angels that followed him.

- In 1 Thessalonians 4:16, we are told more:

✞ **1 Thessalonians 4:16** "For the Lord Himself will descend from heaven with a shout, with the voice of the archangel and with the trumpet of God, and the dead in Christ will rise first."

  ~ The word "archangel" is used nowhere else in the New Testament, except for Jude 9 applying to Michael.
  ~ "Archangel" means "chief angel; one who is first, or who is over others."
    * In the Revelation passage, we learned that Michael had angels under him.

3. Satan (serpent, Devil) rebelled and desires to **DECEIVE** men.

- There are many names for Satan, including "the devil" and "the serpent."
- Who tempted Eve in the Garden of Eden? The serpent. (Genesis 3:1–5)
  ~ God prophesied after the Fall that the serpent would "bruise Jesus' heel, but Jesus would bruise his head." (Genesis 3:15)
- In Revelation 12:9a Satan's various names are given and his main goal revealed:

✞ **Revelation 12:9a** "And the great dragon was thrown down, the serpent of old who is called the devil and Satan, who deceives the whole world ..."

  ~ His names: great dragon, serpent of old, the devil, and Satan.
  ~ His goal: deceive the whole world.

- We can learn more about Satan in Ezekiel 28:12–15.
  ~ He was perfect in all his ways on the day he was created.
  ~ He was beautiful.
  ~ He was full of wisdom.
  ~ He had an important job—to guard (cover) the throne room of God.
  ~ He was blameless in his ways ... UNTIL ...
  ~ Unrighteousness was found in him.

- In Isaiah 14:11–14 God explained "why" Satan was found unrighteous.

~ The repetitive phrase in these verses is "I will" (the "I" is Satan).

* I will ascend to heaven.
* I will raise my throne above the stars of God.
* I will sit on the mount of assembly.
* I will ascend above the heights of the clouds.
* I will make myself like the Most High.

⇨ **Satan became focused on "self" and consumed with his own beauty, brawn, and "brains."**

▪ Some believe that Chapter 12 in the book of Revelation explains that one-third of all the angels chose to follow Satan.

~ If that is true, then one-third of 10,000 times 10,000 and thousands of thousands angels followed him—that is a lot of bad angels.

~ The good news is that there are twice as many good angels as bad.

> ★ **TEACHING TIP:**
> *The absolute tragedy is not only did Adam and Eve lose a perfect, close intimacy with God—but the only thing they gained was the knowledge of evil! Such is the vile nature of Satan's deception!*

▪ As the book of Revelation states, Satan desires to deceive men. How?

▪ One of the best examples is found in the exchange between Eve and Satan in the Garden of Eden. (Genesis 3: 1–5) Look at Satan's tactics regarding the one tree from which God had forbidden Adam and Eve to eat.

~ First: He cast <u>doubt</u> regarding God's Word—*"Did He (God) say that?"*

~ Second: He <u>denied</u> what God had said—*"Surely you will not die."*

~ Third: He <u>replaced</u> God's Word by questioning God's character—*"For God knows...you will be like God, knowing good and evil."*

> ★ **TEACHING TIP:**
> *Remember the apostle Paul's words—Satan will appear as an angel of light. (2 Corinthians 11:14) In other words, Satan can come looking "good" to the undiscerning.*

▪ Jude wanted his readers to understand:

~ Satan is a liar.

~ His battle is against God because he hates what God loves: Israel and the church.

4. God gave two weapons to fight Satan: the <u>WORD</u> of God and the <u>NAME</u> of God.

▪ When Jesus dealt with Satan in the wilderness, how did He respond? He used Scripture, God's Word.

JUDE
Theme: Contend for the Faith

   ~ He stated, "It is written …"

- When Michael disputed with the devil over Moses' body, he brought in God as his authority saying, "The Lord rebuke you."

- Believers have two weapons for their battle against Satan:
  (1) The Word of God

✝ **Hebrews 4:12** "For the word of God is living and active and sharper than any two-edged sword, and piercing as far as the division of soul and spirit, of both joints and marrow, and able to judge the thoughts and intentions of the heart."

    (2) The Name of God

✝ **Jeremiah 10:6** "There is none like You, O Lord; You are great, and great is Your name in might."

****

❋ **ILLUSTRATION:** A woman walked alone down the beach—it was off-season and no one was around. She was enjoying her solitude until she realized that a young man had come up beside her and he was unclothed. Given the circumstances, she became nervous and decided to turn around and head home.

As she went to turn, the man grabbed her. In great fear, she turned to him and said, "The Lord Jesus rebuke you!" The man let her go and ran from her.

The woman was stunned, but shared that she remembered the archangel Michael saying to the devil, "The Lord rebuke you!" She decided that she probably should not have been shocked that the man released her and ran away because there is power in the name of Jesus.

****

Lesson #2: Satan must be fought with God's authority, not our own.

  C. Jude gave three examples of the motives of apostates and the consequences:

✝ **Jude 11** "Woe to them! For they have gone the way of Cain, and for pay they have rushed headlong into the error of Balaam, and perished in the rebellion of Korah."

    1. The way of Cain—<u>SELF</u>-righteous religion of trusting own works. Cain departed from the presence of the Lord.

- In Genesis 4, we studied how Cain, a "tiller of the ground," brought an offering to the Lord of fruit of the ground, but God did not accept it. God did, however, accept Abel's offering of a "firstling of his flock" (a lamb).
- Cain responded to God in anger, even though God offered him a second opportunity to present an acceptable offering.
- Instead, Cain's anger led to him murdering his brother, Abel.

- Cain wanted to approach God with an offering that he, Cain, found acceptable—the work of his own hands.
  - ~ In fact, he refused the second chance God gave him to get this right.
- Cain's pride was not only self-righteous, but it was self-destructive and also led to the murder of an innocent bystander, Abel.

- In a worldly sense, Cain would be considered successful because he built a city.
- But God sent him from His presence. Therefore, Cain never experienced any eternal accomplishment.

2. **The error of Balaam—<u>GREED</u> or religion for material gain. Balaam was killed by the sword.**

<u>Numbers 22–24</u>
- When Israel was going into the Promised Land, they "conquered" their way in.
- The king of Moab, King Balak, sent for the prophet Balaam (a prophet for hire) and told him, "I will pay you to come and curse Israel."
- But God spoke to Balaam and told him—do not go with Moab's men, do not listen to them, and do not curse the ones I have blessed. So Balaam sent Moab's men away.
- Moab sent another delegation offering Balaam riches and power—things that appealed to Balaam. He could be motivated by greed, speaking religious words for monetary gain.
- Balaam responded that he would pray and ask God again—as if God would change His mind or heart about His people. God responded, "… only the word which I speak to you shall you do." (Numbers 22:20)
- But without God's direction, Balaam went with King Balak's men. God used a talking donkey and an angel to warn Balaam to stop.
- Ultimately, Balaam could only speak God's words and was unable to curse the Israelites but his evil ways toward God's people were not finished.

- In Revelation 2:14, we are told how Balaam kept teaching Balak:
  - ~ To put a stumbling block before the sons of Israel.
    - * To get them to eat things sacrificed to idols.
    - * To get them to commit acts of immorality.

- In other words, Balaam attempted to use his knowledge to defeat the very prophesies he had spoken!
- Balaam set himself against God's chosen people and he was killed by the sword. (Numbers 31:8)

3. The rebellion of Korah—<u>RESISTING</u> the authority God has given another. Korah perished.

<u>Numbers 16:1–32</u>
- Moses had been chosen by God to lead the people of Israel.
- Korah, a Levite, challenged Moses' authority with the express desire to usurp it:

✞ **Numbers 16:3** "They assembled together against Moses and Aaron, and said to them, 'You have gone far enough, for all the congregation are holy, every one of them, and the Lord is in their midst; so why do you exalt yourselves above the assembly of the Lord?'"

- Korah's rebellion against Moses was actually an act of resisting the authority that God had given another person.
- What made Korah's attitude and action all the more grievous was that he gathered others to defy Moses and Aaron—which meant they were participants in a mutiny against God.
- Ultimately their defiant actions led to Korah's and their demise—all were swallowed up by the ground. (Numbers 16:32)

D. False teachers are dangerous, useless, fruitless, and doomed for <u>DESTRUCTION</u>.

- Jude gave illustrations from nature to describe false teachers:
✞ **Jude 12–13** "These are the men who are hidden reefs in your love feasts when they feast with you without fear, caring for themselves; clouds without water, carried along by winds; autumn trees without fruit, doubly dead, uprooted; wild waves of the sea, casting up their own shame like foam; wandering stars, for whom the black darkness has been reserved forever."
  - ~ Hidden reefs: If you are in a boat, a hidden reef can be dangerous. Something "hidden" can hit you and sink you quickly.
  - ~ Clouds without water: These are useless clouds. A cloud is supposed to have water to bring rain to the earth.
  - ~ Autumn trees without fruit: In other words, they are fruitless.
  - ~ Wandering stars reserved for darkness: A falling star is just going to burn up.
- What point was Jude trying to make with these "visuals?" False teachers are:

~ Dangerous
~ Useless
~ Fruitless
~ Doomed for destruction

Jude 14–16

- Jude continued his train of thought by speaking of Enoch—who was taken to heaven by God, thus never physically dying.
  - ~ Jude explained that Enoch had prophesied that the Lord was coming and coming to execute judgment on the ungodly ones.
- Interesting to note, the term "godly sinners" means "despisers of God, impious."

III. DEFENSE AGAINST FALSE TEACHERS: DUTY OF THE BELIEVERS (JUDE 17–23)

A. Contend for the faith by REMEMBERING the Word's warning about false teachers.

- Jude turned from the destructive plight of the false teachers to speak to the believers with an important word—*REMEMBER*!

> ✠ **Jude 17–20** "But you, beloved, ought to remember the words that were spoken beforehand by the apostles of our Lord Jesus Christ, that they were saying to you, 'In the last time there will be mockers, following after their own ungodly lusts.' These are the ones who cause divisions, worldly-minded, devoid of the Spirit."

★ **TEACHING TIP:**
It is paramount that believers know God's Word for themselves!

- Remember:
  - ~ The words of the apostles that warned of false teachers to come.
  - ~ That the false teachers would be ungodly.
  - ~ That the false teachers would cause divisions within the church.
  - ~ That the false teachers would be devoid of the Holy Spirit.

****

❋ **ILLUSTRATION:** A couple visited a new Sunday school class in their church. They had heard about a teacher who was very bright, articulate, and challenged the class members' "traditional" way of thinking. Members referred to him as a "great communicator." As the couple sat in the class, they became more and more alarmed as they listened to true Biblical doctrine being questioned. The teacher seemed to suggest that the Word was antiquated and no longer relevant—a false doctrine was presented as being more "enlightened." Finally, they could stay silent no longer and questioned the teacher and his

approach. To their utter amazement, he smiled and responded, "I like to teach as a devil's advocate." They responded, "Whose advocate? The devil?" The room fell silent as that statement hung in the air. The problem was that he had been succeeding for some time as the devil's advocate within the church.

****

B. Build yourself up in the faith by <u>PRAYING</u> in the Holy Spirit.

✝ **Jude 20** "But you, beloved, building yourselves up on your most holy faith, praying in the Holy Spirit …"

- John had reminded them that the false teachers were "devoid" of the Spirit.
- Believers are to pray to God in the Spirit—to continue to grow spiritually.
- When believers are faithful to prayer, they are more mindful of obedience to God's Word and of looking forward to Christ's return.

C. Keep yourself in God's love by <u>OBEYING</u> (See John 15:10).

Jude 21 "… keep yourselves in the love of God, waiting anxiously for the mercy of our Lord Jesus Christ to eternal life."

> ★ **TEACHING TIP:**
> *Our own strength will not keep us eternally secure—only God's love can do that.*

- Go back to the first verse in this book—it states that we are "kept by Jesus."
  - ~ Once we accept Him as our Savior and Lord, we are secure in Jesus.
  - ~ BUT we need to keep ourselves in His love.
- Jesus was very clear in our cross-reference:

✝ **John 15:10** "If you keep My commandments, you will abide in My love; just as I have kept My Father's commandments and abide in His love."

> **NOTE:** Consider the prodigal son:
> - What did he do? He left his father's love.
> - Did his father love him? Yes, yes, and yes.
> - But the prodigal did not abide in his father's love.
>
> ⇨ **When we refuse to obey God and His Word, we, in effect, are no longer abiding in His love—we, like the prodigal, have run away from it.**

JUDE
Theme: Contend for the Faith

- Jude called believers to have mercy on some who doubted—but to exhibit such mercy with fear.

✝ **Jude 22–23** "And have mercy on some, who are doubting; save others, snatching them out of the fire; and on some have mercy with fear, hating even the garment polluted by the flesh."
  ~ The word "fear" in this context means "with caution."
- In others words, if you see another believer falling for untruth being touted by the false teachers, then you need to help them—with caution.
- Why "with caution?" Because we do not want to somehow be lured into the same unbelief that they have and also fall for untruth.

IV. VICTORY OVER FALSE TEACHERS (JUDE 24–25)

A. Only Jesus is able to keep you from **STUMBLING**.

- Jesus can do this because He is God.
- He is watching over us, guarding us, keeping us from falling into the snares of the false teachers and their error.
- And He will do this for us until the end! Amen!

> ★ **TEACHING TIP:**
> *Three of the sweetest, most powerful words in Scripture to remember: HE IS ABLE!*

B. Jesus is **GOD** our Savior with glory, majesty, and authority.

- And because of this very fact, this very truth, we have been rescued and redeemed!
  ~ Saved from sin and death.
  ~ Experiencing a great exchange that promises heaven as our eternal home.

Lesson #3: Jesus, who keeps the apostate for judgment, keeps us from falling.

FINAL THOUGHTS AND APPLICATION

⌘ Jude made the case to contend for the faith.

⌘ In order to contend for the faith, we must know certain truths that Jude laid out:
  ~ False teachers are real.
  ~ Satan is real.
  ~ Jesus is real and He is the only One who can keep us from falling into the untruth of Satan.
  ~ Jesus is coming. He is coming to judge.

JUDE
Theme: Contend for the Faith

⌑ Believers must be strong and continue to grow spiritually, in order to contend (wrestle, agonize) over the faith.

****

❋ **ILLUSTRATION:** Have you ever encountered drivers who are ready to contend over a piece of highway? A couple came to a four-way stop sign at the same time as another driver. The couple went through first, which enraged the other driver who apparently wanted to go through the four-way stop first. The driver followed the couple for miles—swearing at them, gesturing inappropriately, and even trying to run them off the road! He was passionate—he was ready to wrestle over a thoroughfare.

This driver is not someone you would want to emulate. But don't miss the point—he was passionate about his position.

****

⌑ Jude wanted to motivate believers to be ready and willing to contend for the faith—even if it proved to be an agonizing endeavor. The faith—Jesus Christ—is worth it!

❖ **FINAL APPLICATION: Are you contending for the faith, trusting that Jesus is all you need to win the battle?**

JUDE REVIEW HELPS

⌂ Put the names of all the books that have been studied from Genesis to Revelation on cards.

⌂ Give each person several cards and have them work as a team to put the cards around the room in sequential order.

⌂ After they have done that, have them identify which books were in what sets:

- ◆ The Pentateuch

- ◆ Kingdom Books

- ◆ Post-Exilic Books

- ◆ Poetical Books

- ◆ Major Prophets

- ◆ Early Minor Prophets

- ◆ Later Minor Prophets

- ◆ New Testament Historical Books

- ◆ Paul's Letters to the Churches

- ◆ Paul's Letters to Pastors

- ◆ Other Letters and Revelation

JUDE REVIEW HELPS

¤ **Put the names of all the books that have been studied from Genesis to Revelation on cards.**

¤ **Give each person several cards and have them work as a team to put the cards around the room in sequential order.**

¤ **After they have done that, have them identify which books were in what sets:**

- ◆ **The Pentateuch**
  Genesis, Exodus, Leviticus, Numbers, Deuteronomy

- ◆ **Kingdom Books**
  Joshua, Judges, Ruth, 1 Samuel, 2 Samuel, 1 Kings, 2 Kings

- ◆ **Post-Exilic Books**
  1 Chronicles, 2 Chronicles, Ezra, Nehemiah, Esther

- ◆ **Poetical Books**
  Job, Psalms, Proverbs, Ecclesiastes, Song of Solomon

- ◆ **Major Prophets**
  Isaiah, Jeremiah, Lamentations, Ezekiel, Daniel

- ◆ **Early Minor Prophets**
  Hosea, Joel, Amos, Obadiah, Jonah, Micah

- ◆ **Later Minor Prophets**
  Nahum, Habakkuk, Zephaniah, Haggai, Zechariah, Malachi

- ◆ **New Testament Historical Books**
  Matthew, Mark, Luke, John, Acts

- ◆ **Paul's Letters to the Churches**
  Romans, 1 Corinthians, 2 Corinthians, Galatians, Ephesians, Philippians, Colossians, 1 Thessalonians, 2 Thessalonians

- ◆ **Paul's Letters to Pastors**
  1 Timothy, 2 Timothy, Titus, Philemon

- ◆ **Other Letters and Revelation**
  Hebrews, James, 1 Peter, 2 Peter, 1 John, 2 John, 3 John, Jude, Revelation

REVELATION

God's Final Victory

Therefore write the things which you have seen,

and the things which are, and the things

which will take place after these things.

Revelation 1:19

SESSION SIXTY-SIX: REVELATION
God's Final Victory

✝ **Memory verse:** *"Therefore write the things which you have seen, and the things which are, and the things which will take place after these things."* *(Revelation 1:19)*

Introduction: A war began in Genesis 3 when man rebelled against God. As soon as sin entered the world, God gave a promise that He would send someone to save men from their sins. He did that a few thousand years later when He sent Christ as the suffering servant. But there were also promises of the King of Kings returning and dealing a death blow to Satan and the evil in this world. In the book of Revelation, John lays out God's plan for the end times and for the coming of the Lord. It is the culmination of the plan for redemption. The King will come and bring His Kingdom, where believers will live with Him for all eternity. Amen!

- **Oral Review:** There is no **REVIEW** for this week.

- **Homework:** Review the homework from the book of Jude.

    Question on page 203
    Questions on pages 205–206
    Questions on pages 208–209
    Questions on pages 211–212

- **Review Helps:** Written review is provided at the end of the teacher presentation. (Optional and time permitting.)

- **Teacher Presentation on the Book of Revelation**

- **Learning for Life:** You may choose to discuss all or just one or two of the questions on page 225.

- **Closing prayer:** Pray that the earnest and sincere prayer of each student would be John's poignant cry, "Come, Lord Jesus!" and that they would look with great anticipation and joy to the coming of our Lord Jesus, King of Kings and Lord of Lords.

REVELATION
Theme: God's Final Victory

OUTLINE AID FOR TEACHERS:

I. THE INTRODUCTION

A. Revelation can be interpreted in <u>FOUR</u> ways.

    1. The <u>PRETERIST</u> interpretation views the prophecies as having been fulfilled during the time John lived.

    2. The <u>HISTORICAL</u> interpretation sees the book as a panorama of church history from John's time until the end times.

    3. The <u>IDEALIST</u> interprets the book as principles of conflict between good and evil, not actual events.

    4. The <u>FUTURIST</u> interprets the prophecies plainly as yet to be fulfilled.

B. The visions were given to the apostle <u>JOHN</u>.

    1. He was exiled to <u>PATMOS</u> probably around A.D. 95–96 during Domitian's reign as emperor of Rome.

    2. Revelation is the only New Testament book of <u>PROPHECY</u>.

    3. It is the only book that promises a <u>BLESSING</u> on those who read it. (Revelation 1:3)

II. JOHN'S VISION OF CHRIST: "THE THINGS WHICH YOU HAVE SEEN" (REVELATION 1)

A. Christ's appearance in His <u>GLORIFIED</u> body is described.

    1. He is clothed in a robe with a <u>GOLDEN</u> belt.

    2. His hair is <u>WHITE</u> as wool.

    3. His eyes are like a <u>FLAME</u> of fire.

    4. His feet are like burnished <u>BRONZE</u>.

    5. His voice is like the sound of <u>MANY</u> waters.

    6. His face is like the <u>SUN</u> shining in its strength.

    7. From His mouth comes a sharp two-edged <u>SWORD</u>.

REVELATION
Theme: God's Final Victory

B. Seven <u>LAMPSTANDS</u> represent the seven churches.

C. The seven <u>STARS</u> in His hand represent the seven angels of the churches.

III. **JOHN'S RECORDING OF CHRIST'S MESSAGES TO THE SEVEN CHURCHES: "THE THINGS WHICH ARE" (REVELATION 2–3)**

A. Ephesus: You have left your first <u>LOVE</u>.

B. Smyrna: You are poor, but you are <u>RICH</u>.

C. Pergamum: You hold to the teachings of <u>BALAAM</u>.

D. Thyatira: You tolerate evil <u>TEACHERS</u>.

E. Sardis: You have a name that you are alive, but you are <u>DEAD</u>.

F. Philadelphia: You have kept the <u>WORD</u> and have not denied Christ's name.

G. Laodicea: You are neither hot nor cold. I will <u>SPIT</u> you out of My mouth.

IV. **JOHN'S VISIONS OF THE FUTURE: "THE THINGS WHICH WILL TAKE PLACE (REVELATION 4–22)**

A. The scene in <u>HEAVEN</u> is described.

B. The Lamb is <u>COMMISSIONED</u>.

C. The seven <u>SEALS</u> are opened.

1. Seal One: There will be <u>CONQUEST</u>.

2. Seal Two: There will be <u>WAR</u>.

3. Seal Three: There will be <u>FAMINE</u>.

4. Seal Four: One-fourth of the earth will <u>DIE</u>.

5. Seal Five: There will be a cry from the <u>MARTYRS</u>.

6. Seal Six: There will be a <u>COSMIC</u> upheaval.

Interlude: 144,000 <u>JEWISH</u> bond-servants will be sealed.

7. Seal Seven: There will be <u>SILENCE</u> in heaven, and then the seven trumpets prepare to sound.

REVELATION
Theme: God's Final Victory

   D.   The seven <u>TRUMPETS</u> are sounded.

     1.   Trumpet One: One-third of the <u>EARTH</u> is burned up.

     2.   Trumpet Two: One-third of the <u>SEA</u> becomes blood.

     3.   Trumpet Three: One-third of fresh <u>RIVERS</u> become poisonous.

     4.   Trumpet Four: One-third of <u>HEAVENLY</u> bodies are darkened.

     5.   Trumpet Five: <u>LOCUSTS</u> are sent to torment men.

     6.   Trumpet Six: One-third of mankind is <u>KILLED</u>.

Interlude: John eats a <u>SCROLL</u>; the two witnesses are killed in Jerusalem.

     7.   Trumpet Seven: The kingdom of God on earth is <u>PROCLAIMED</u>!

   E.   The seven <u>BOWL</u> judgments are poured out.

     1.   Bowl One: Malignant <u>SORES</u> are upon those who worship the beast.

     2.   Bowl Two: The sea becomes <u>BLOOD</u> and everything in it dies.

     3.   Bowl Three: All <u>RIVERS</u> and springs become blood.

     4.   Bowl Four: The sun <u>SCORCHES</u> men.

     5.   Bowl Five: All becomes <u>DARK</u>.

     6.   Bowl Six: The Euphrates <u>DRIES</u> up; nations gather for war.

     7.   Bowl Seven: It is <u>DONE</u>; the wrath of God is complete.

   F.   The second coming of Christ is described.

     1.   Christ's coming is <u>ANNOUNCED</u>.

     2.   Christ comes with His <u>ARMIES</u>.

     3.   Christ is <u>VICTORIOUS</u>.

   G.   The millennial <u>KINGDOM</u> is established on earth for one thousand years.

   H.   The <u>NEW</u> Jerusalem is described as coming down from heaven, the eternal home for those whose names are written in the Book of Life.

REVELATION
[God's Final Victory]

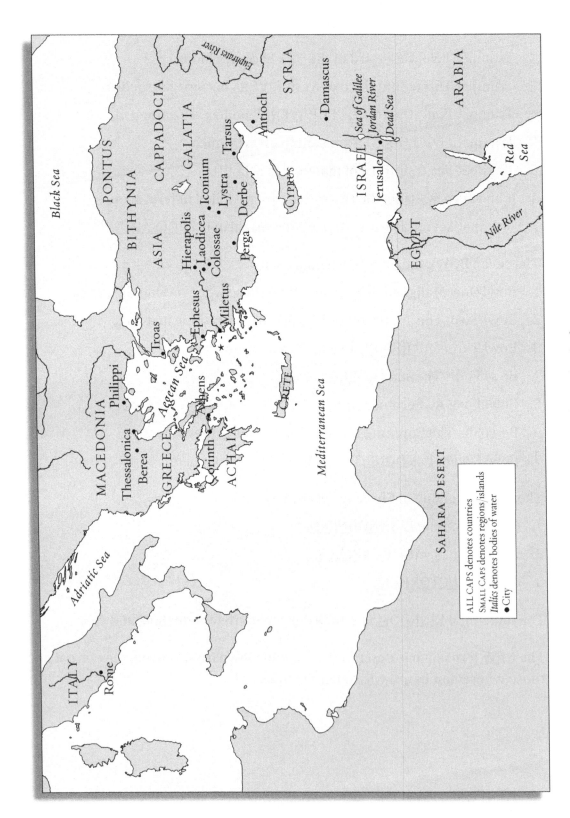

ALL CAPS denotes countries
SMALL CAPS denotes regions/islands
Italics denotes bodies of water
●City

* Indicates location of the island of Patmos

REVELATION
Theme: God's Final Victory

THE BASICS:
⇨ **Who: The Author:** John
⇨ **What:** The revelation of Jesus Christ
⇨ **When:** Written around A.D. 95–96
⇨ **Where:** Written from the island of Patmos to the churches in Asia
⇨ **Why:** To record what John has seen, what is, and what is to come; it is the final victory of Jesus Christ

MEMORY VERSE: *"Therefore write the things which you have seen, and the things which are, and the things which will take place after these things." Revelation 1:19*

****

REVIEW:
⌶ The *Old Testament History* books addressed sin, judgment, and death (the consequences of sin), and the promised Messiah.

⌶ The *New Testament History* books addressed Jesus' first coming, His time on earth, and the birth of the church.

⌶ In *Paul's Letters to the Churches*, Paul addressed the following:
~ **Romans:** God's righteousness described.
~ **First Corinthians:** Church's problems corrected.
~ **Second Corinthians:** Paul's ministry defended.
~ **Galatians:** Believers' freedom in Christ.
~ **Ephesians:** Believers' holy walk.
~ **Philippians:** Believers' joy in Christ.
~ **Colossians:** Believers' completion in Christ.
~ **First Thessalonians:** The return of the Lord.
~ **Second Thessalonians:** The Day of the Lord.

⌶ In *Paul's Letters to Pastors*, Paul addressed the following:
~ **First Timothy:** Instructions on leadership.
~ **Second Timothy:** Instructions on endurance.
~ **Titus:** Instructions on church order.
~ **Philemon:** Instructions on forgiveness.

⌶ In *Other Letters and Revelation*, the authors addressed:
~ **Hebrews:** Christ's superiority.
~ **James:** Live faith through works.
~ **First Peter:** Suffer steadfastly.

REVELATION
Theme: God's Final Victory

- **Second Peter:** Identify false teachers.
- **First John:** Fellowship with God.
- **Second John:** Shun false teachers.
- **Third John:** Show hospitality.
- **Jude:** Contend for the faith.

OVERVIEW:

- We have reached the final book of God's story—and we will see a celebration as the bride at last joins her groom.
- But, before we can celebrate, we will look together at difficult times.

****

✻ **ILLUSTRATION:** World War II started in 1939. People at the time thought, as they did during World War I, "Perhaps we can have this one last war. We can get through it and we will be done with war forever." World War II lasted for approximately six years. In the end, there was hope, but it did not last long because conflicts once again began and continue into our present day—even though the hearts of men and women long for peace.

The war isn't just raging between countries—it rages within every man, woman, and child. The war is with our sin nature. The war is with the attacks of Satan. This battle has been going on since the beginning of time, starting with Adam and Eve when they decided to be their own little 'g' god—sin entered the world and there has been conflict ever since.

****

⇨ **The purpose of the book of Revelation was to announce God's final victory!**

I.   THE INTRODUCTION

- The book of Revelation is the very last book in the Word of God.
- It is not an easy book to study—it has kept great scholars somewhat perplexed for hundreds of years.
- It is a book that is quite mysterious.
    - There are over three hundred symbols in it.
    - There are at least four different ways to interpret it.

A. Revelation can be interpreted in <u>FOUR</u> ways.

- These interpretations come from many wise, very bright, and very intelligent scholars.

REVELATION
Theme: God's Final Victory

- These commentators have studied Revelation and believe that they have evidence that supports their particular interpretation.

  ### 1. The <u>PRETERIST</u> interpretation views the prophecies as having been fulfilled during the time John lived.

- John lived during a difficult time in history, so they believe that all the events in Revelation have taken place.

  ### 2. The <u>HISTORICAL</u> interpretation sees the book as a panorama of church history from John's time until the end times.

- They believe that some of the events have already taken place and others will take place in the future.
- They believe that all of the events in Revelation take place over the entire course of the history of the church and will end at the end times.

  ### 3. The <u>IDEALIST</u> interprets the book as principles of conflict between good and evil, not actual events.

- They disagree with the first two, stating that Revelation is not about real, tangible events.
- Their interpretation is more of a poetical viewpoint.

  ### 4. The <u>FUTURIST</u> interprets the prophecies plainly as yet to be fulfilled.

- They believe that all of the events in Revelation will occur in the future and over a short period of time.

⇨ **For our study, we will take the "futurist" viewpoint and look at the Scriptures as they are plainly stated in the Bible.**

B. The visions were given to the apostle <u>JOHN</u>.

- There is also debate over his authorship, but most commentators agree it was the apostle John who also wrote the books of John and 1, 2, and 3 John.
- John walked with Jesus Christ.
- This is a vision that Jesus gave to him.

  ### 1. He was exiled to <u>PATMOS</u> probably around A.D. 95–96 during Domitian's reign as emperor of Rome.

REVELATION
Theme: God's Final Victory

- The island of Patmos was not a resort. It was a prison island and John was there as a criminal.
  - ~ He was there because he had not been able to stay quiet about Jesus Christ.
- There was little on the island, except mining; and John probably worked in the mines.

- He was probably close to ninety years old during this time.

- It is believed that John was on Patmos during the rule of Domitian in Rome.
  - ~ There are those who think that it was perhaps Nero who reigned during this time.
  - ~ But the timeline would suggest that Domitian was in control.

> ★ **TEACHING TIP:**
> *Both Nero and Domitian were cruel leaders.*

2. Revelation is the only New Testament book of <u>PROPHECY</u>.

- There is other prophecy in the New Testament, but it comes in "bits and pieces," whereas Revelation is almost entirely prophecy.

3. It is the only book that promises a <u>BLESSING</u> on those who read it. (Revelation 1:3)

✝ **Revelation 1:3** "Blessed is he who reads and those who hear the words of the prophecy, and heed the things which are written in it; for the time is near."

- It is the only book that promises a blessing to its readers—who read it, hear it, and heed it.

- Jesus instructed John on what to write:

✝ **Revelation 1:19** "Therefore write the things which you have seen, and the things which are, and the things which will take place after these things."
  - ~ What you have seen: John had seen the glorified Jesus Christ before him.
  - ~ Things which are: the messages to the church.
  - ~ Things which will take place after these things: future things (events) to come.

- The word "revelation" means the "unveiling of something hidden."
- Jesus was about to "unveil" that which was "hidden" to John.

- In Revelation 1:9–13 John explained the scene:
  - ~ He was on the island of Patmos.
  - ~ It was the day of the Lord (probably the Sabbath day).
  - ~ John was in the Spirit, worshiping God.

REVELATION
Theme: God's Final Victory

- ~ He heard a voice behind him that sounded like a trumpet.
- ~ He turned to find someone like the son of man standing there—Jesus Christ.

- ▪ The last time John had seen Jesus Christ was on Mount Olivet when Jesus had met with His disciples. (Acts 1:6–9)
  - ~ Jesus told them that He was leaving, but the Holy Spirit would come upon them.
  - ~ Jesus told them that they would be witnesses to all the nations.
  - ~ Jesus then ascended into heaven.
- ▪ Jesus had been a carpenter, a minister, God on earth in human form, and a resurrected Savior. John last saw Him as He ascended into heaven.

> **NOTE:** John, after years of longing to see his dearest friend again, was face-to-face with Jesus in His heavenly, glorified body. What an incredible, amazing reunion!

- ▪ John was at first very afraid, but then Jesus reached out to him:
- ✞ **Revelation 1:17** "When I saw Him, I fell at His feet like a dead man. And He placed His right hand on me, saying, 'Do not be afraid; I am the first and the last …'"

II. JOHN'S VISION OF CHRIST: "THE THINGS WHICH YOU HAVE SEEN" (REVELATION 1)

A. Christ's appearance in His <u>GLORIFIED</u> body is described.

<u>Revelation 1:13–16</u>
- ▪ His appearance was something immensely unusual—brilliant and magnificent.

  1. **He is clothed in a robe with a <u>GOLDEN</u> belt.**

  2. **His hair is <u>WHITE</u> as wool.**

  3. **His eyes are like a <u>FLAME</u> of fire.**

  4. **His feet are like burnished <u>BRONZE</u>.**

  5. **His voice is like the sound of <u>MANY</u> waters.**

  6. **His face is like the <u>SUN</u> shining in its strength.**

  7. **From His mouth comes a sharp two-edged <u>SWORD</u>.**

REVELATION
Theme: God's Final Victory

- ▪ John also saw seven lampstands and seven stars—Jesus explained what they represented.
- ✟ **Revelation 1:20** "As for the mystery of the seven stars which you saw in My right hand, and the seven golden lampstands: the seven stars are the angels of the seven churches, and the seven lampstands are the seven churches."

B. Seven <u>LAMPSTANDS</u> represent the seven churches.

- ▪ These seven churches could have been churches for which John was the bishop.
- ▪ They could have been seven churches to which John ministered.
- ▪ Jesus will give John a specific message for each of these churches.

> **★ TEACHING TIP:**
> *It is comforting to think that our churches have angels watching them.*

C. The seven <u>STARS</u> in His hand represent the seven angels of the churches.

III.   JOHN'S RECORDING OF CHRIST'S MESSAGES TO THE SEVEN CHURCHES: "THINGS WHICH ARE" (REVELATION 2–3)

> **★ TEACHING TIP:**
> *If one message does not fit your church, keep reading!*

- ▪ These messages are highly relevant for churches today—one of these messages will fit every church.
- ▪ We believe that these are universal messages.

Revelation 2:1–7

A. Ephesus: You have left your first <u>LOVE</u>.

- ▪ Do you remember when the apostle Paul wrote Ephesus? He commended them because they had a great love for Christ and one another.
- ▪ Thirty years have now passed and the church no longer loved as they had or should.

REVELATION
Theme: God's Final Victory

✝ **Revelation 2:4–5** "But I have this against you, that you have left your first love. Therefore remember from where you have fallen, and repent and do the deeds you did at first; or else I am coming to you and will remove your lampstand out of its place — unless you repent."

> ❖ **APPLICATION:** It is very important in our churches today that we not only totally and devotedly love Jesus, but that we love one another.

Revelation 2:8–11

B. Smyrna: You are poor, but you are <u>RICH</u>.

- This message demonstrates that Jesus does not look at churches in the same way that we do.

✝ **Revelation 2:9a** "I know your tribulation and your poverty (but you are rich) …"
- Jesus stated that others may think they were poor but He knew that they were rich.
  - ~ It would seem that this church had very little money and was struggling to get by.
  - ~ But they were rich in the favor of God.
- Jesus exhorted this church to persevere!

> ★ **TEACHING TIP:**
> *"It [Smyrna] is, however, the only church of the seven which survived, and perhaps in the end its poverty was no disadvantage."*
> *~ Barnes' Notes*

Revelation 2:12–17

C. Pergamum: You hold to the teachings of <u>BALAAM</u>.

- The teachings of Balaam were religious work for financial gain.
- The people seemed to find such teaching/approach to be acceptable, thus did not address it or deal with it.

Revelation 2:18–29

D. Thyatira: You tolerate evil <u>TEACHERS</u>.

- This church tolerated teachers who promoted immorality.
- The teacher named was called Jezebel.
  - ~ A name for someone who is immoral.
- The people were not serious about keeping their church pure.

> ★ **TEACHING TIP:**
> *Throughout the New Testament, the message has been strong and clear about immorality in the church: do not tolerate immoral teachers!*

REVELATION
Theme: God's Final Victory

Revelation 3:1–6

E. Sardis: You have a name that you are alive, but you are <u>DEAD</u>.

- Everyone in the community believed that this church was alive because they:
  - ~ were doing great works.
  - ~ had a lot of money.
  - ~ had a big physical church building.

- Sardis was a church with "works" but not much "life" and what life they had was waning.

★ **TEACHING TIP:**

Sardis had a "reputation without reality."
~ G. Campbell Morgan

Revelation 3:7–13

F. Philadelphia: You have kept the <u>WORD</u> and have not denied Christ's name.

- This church did two things that pleased the Lord:
  1. They kept His Word—obedient.
  2. They did not deny His name—steadfastly faithful.
- Jesus was basically saying to this church, "Well done!"

★ **TEACHING TIP:**

One can only imagine how Christ was lifted up and exalted by their service, worship, obedience, faithfulness—hearts turned heavenward!

Revelation 3:14–22

G. Laodicea: You are neither hot nor cold. I will <u>SPIT</u> you out of My mouth.

- This was a very clear message with a frightening visual!
- God does NOT want a church to be lukewarm toward Him—period.
- A church that is lukewarm leaves Christ "outside."
  - ~ He is not included in their church planning or programs.
  - ~ Most importantly, He is not found in their hearts.

★ **TEACHING TIP:**

Do you want your spouse to love you with a "lukewarm" heart? That would not be real love. Rather, you want your spouse to be excited about you—"on fire" for your relationship.

IV. JOHN'S VISIONS OF THE FUTURE: "THE THINGS WHICH WILL TAKE PLACE" (REVELATION 4–22)

- After finishing His message to the churches, Jesus told John to come with Him.
- John looked up and there was a door opened to heaven.

REVELATION
Theme: God's Final Victory

A. The scene in <u>HEAVEN</u> is described.

<u>Revelation 4:2–11</u>
- There was a throne standing in heaven and One sitting on the throne.
- The One sitting was like a jasper stone and a sardius (a red precious stone, probably a ruby or carnelian) in appearance.
- There was a rainbow around the throne that was like an emerald in appearance.
- There were twenty-four thrones around the main throne.
- On those thrones were seated elders in white robes with crowns on their heads.

- There were four living creatures with unusual appearances but all worshiping the Most High God.
  - ~ The first: like a lion.
  - ~ The second: like a calf.
  - ~ The third: a face like that of a man.
  - ~ The fourth: like a flying eagle.
- An incredible scene of worship was taking place as the elders, the four living creatures, and all of the angels worshiped God Almighty with great joy.

> ✸ **TEACHING TIP:**
> *As you are reading about this, do not miss the times of worship.*

B. The Lamb is <u>COMMISSIONED</u>.

<u>Revelation 5:1–10</u>
- God had a scroll in His hand and He asked a question: "Who is worthy to unseal the scroll?"
- There was silence and no one came forward.
- John must have known that it was terribly important that the scroll be opened because he began to weep—not just a few tears, rather he was greatly weeping. (Revelation 5:4)
- One of the elders spoke to John, "Stop weeping; behold, the Lion that is from the tribe of Judah, the Root of David, has overcome so as to open the book and its seven seals."
- John turned to see a Lamb as if slain—Jesus Christ.

> ✸ **TEACHING TIP:**
> *It is here where we have a picture of Christ being commissioned.*

- Christ came forward and took the scroll with seven seals.
- In opening the sealed book, He would release judgment on the world—on all the evil that has taken place for thousands upon thousands of years.

C. The seven <u>SEALS</u> are opened.

REVELATION
Theme: God's Final Victory

Revelation 6

1. Seal One: There will be <u>CONQUEST</u>.

- When the first seal is opened, a white horse with a rider appears.
- He is sent out to bring conquest to the world.

> **NOTE:** This probably represents unsettledness in the world. Cold wars will take place. All peace in the world will not be taken away, but there will be a stirring up in the earth, especially of hatred.

2. Seal Two: There will be <u>WAR</u>.

- The next horse is red (a color of bloodshed) with a rider seated upon him.
- They were sent out to wage wars—to take peace from the earth.

3. Seal Three: There will be <u>FAMINE</u>.

- The next horse to arrive with a rider is black (suggesting distress and calamity).
- They are sent out to bring famine upon the earth.

4. Seal Four: One-fourth of the earth will <u>DIE</u>.

- The fourth horse is ashen (signifying death)—he and his rider are sent to bring death to the earth.
- One-fourth of all the peoples on the earth will die.

5. Seal Five: There will be a cry from the <u>MARTYRS</u>.

- John's attention is transported back into the throne room.
- He hears the cries of those who were martyred for the name of Christ.
- They cried out to the Father in a loud voice:
✝ **Revelation 6:10** "'How long, O Lord, holy and true, will You refrain from judging and avenging our blood on those who dwell on the earth?'"

- The response to their cries was very unusual. After being dressed in white, they were told:
✝ **Revelation 6:11b** "... and they were told that they should rest for a little while longer, until the number of their fellow servants and their brethren who were to be killed even as they had been, would be completed also."
    ~ In other words, all of the believers who need to be martyred have not been martyred *yet*.
    ~ They are told that they must wait a little longer.

6. Seal Six: There will be a <u>COSMIC</u> upheaval.

- With the breaking of the sixth seal, the earth is impacted, as if it is being shaken.
  - ~ An enormous earthquake.
  - ~ A cataclysmic disturbance in the heavenlies.
- People will cry out with a desire to die, but will offer no cries of repentance.

> ★ **TEACHING TIP:**
> *Again—man is crying out but not in repentance.*

Interlude: 144,000 <u>JEWISH</u> bond-servants will be sealed.

Revelation 7:1–8
- Judgment on the earth takes a pause.
- God chooses and seals 144,000 Jews to carry His message to the ends of the earth.
- The "pause" lasts until the bond-servants of God are sealed on their foreheads.
- The total is made up of twelve thousand from each tribe of Israel.

> ★ **TEACHING TIP:**
> *The "sealing" represents God's protection.*

7. Seal Seven: There will be <u>SILENCE</u> in heaven, and then the seven trumpets prepare to sound.

Revelation 8:1–6
- What happens? Nothing.
- There is silence in heaven for one-half hour.
  - ~ There is no worshiping.
  - ~ There is no angelic applause.
- There is nothing but silence as the trumpeters prepare for the seven trumpets.

⇨ **The first round of judgments has been revealed in the seven seals. Now the second round begins with the sounding of the seven trumpets.**

D. The seven <u>TRUMPETS</u> are sounded.

Revelation 8:7–10:11

1. Trumpet One: One-third of the <u>EARTH</u> is burned up.

2. Trumpet Two: One-third of the <u>SEA</u> becomes blood.

> **NOTE:** Does this sound familiar? In our study of the book of Exodus, we learned that Moses touched the river and it became blood.

3. Trumpet Three: One-third of fresh <u>RIVERS</u> become poisonous.

- No one will be able to drink from these waters.

4. Trumpet Four: One-third of <u>HEAVENLY</u> bodies are darkened.

5. Trumpet Five: <u>LOCUSTS</u> are sent to torment men.

Revelation 9:1–11
- John saw these locusts coming up from the abyss.
- They were sent with the sole purpose to torment men who do not have the seal of God on their foreheads—nor were they to cause harm to any living, green thing.
- These locusts are compared to scorpions that are known for their lethal sting.
- However, they were not permitted to kill anyone but to torment them for five months.
- Those who are bitten by these locusts will want to die but won't—instead they will suffer constant agony.

6. Trumpet Six: One-third of mankind is <u>KILLED</u>.

Interlude: John eats a <u>SCROLL</u>; the two witnesses are killed in Jerusalem.

✝ **Revelation 10:9–10** "And he said to me, 'Take it and eat it; it will make your stomach bitter, but in your mouth it will be sweet as honey.' I took the little book out of the angel's hand and ate it, and in my mouth it was sweet as honey; and when I had eaten it, my stomach was made bitter."

> **NOTE:** We, as believers, can get very excited about Christ coming back and about judgment over evil in the world. Yet there is a great sorrow that comes as well, because this is judgment—and we know that judgment is God's way.
> - God has tried for thousands of years to reach people.
> - But people have hardened their hearts toward Him.
> - So what is written for John to eat is sweet in his mouth because evil is at last being judged—but uncomfortable in his stomach because of the sorrow that comes with judgment.

Revelation 11
- Three new characters are introduced.

The Two Witnesses
- The first two introduced are called "two witnesses"—they appear in Jerusalem.
- These two men will be in Jerusalem for three and one-half years.

- During that time they will exhibit unusual powers:
  - ~ They can shut up the sky whenever they decide to.
    - * A "shut sky" produces no rain.
  - ~ They can turn water into blood.
  - ~ They can strike the earth with every plague (if they desire).
  - ~ When people try to kill them (because they are witnessing to Jesus Christ), they will fail because the two men will blow fire out of their mouths and devour their enemies.
- During this period of three and one-half years, no one can touch them.

The Beast
- The third character introduced into the story is "the beast."
- He will come and have the power to kill the two witnesses.
- He will kill them on the streets in Jerusalem and will not bury them. Why won't they be buried?
  - ~ Their death is great news for the people in the world at this point.
  - ~ They will be able to see them on their televisions, computer screens, etc.—the two witnesses are dead, indeed, and lying in the streets of Jerusalem.
- There will be celebrations regarding the witnesses' deaths—gifts will be exchanged (very much like our giving at Christmastime).

- In the midst of the worldwide celebrations—with the two dead men being televised from the streets of Jerusalem—GOD STEPS IN!

✝ **Revelation 11:11–12** "But after the three and a half days, the breath of life from God came into them, and they stood on their feet; and great fear fell upon those who were watching them. And they heard a loud voice from heaven saying to them, 'Come up here.' Then they went up into heaven in the cloud, and their enemies watched them."

- The whole world is watching! And they will witness that God is in control!
  - ~ The two dead witnesses rise up—alive—from God's breathing into them.
  - ~ They ascend into heaven.
  - ~ And fear descends upon those who had been celebrating.

7. Trumpet Seven: The kingdom of God on earth is <u>PROCLAIMED</u>!

- All eyes leave the city of Jerusalem and the two witnesses—John is taken back into the throne room and a turning point takes place:

✝ **Revelation 11:15c** "'... The kingdom of the world has become the kingdom of our Lord and of His Christ; and He will reign forever and ever.'"

REVELATION
Theme: God's Final Victory

✝ **Revelation 11:16–17** "And the twenty-four elders, who sit on their thrones before God, fell on their faces and worshiped God, saying, 'We give You thanks, O Lord God, the Almighty, who are and who were, because You have taken Your great power and have begun to reign.'"

> **NOTE:** Some may be thinking, "I thought He always reigned."
> - Since Adam and Eve sinned in the Garden of Eden, the earth has been Satan's territory.
> - When Satan tempted Jesus in the wilderness, he "offered" the world to Jesus to reign over it—if Jesus would bow to him. Of course, Jesus did not!

- Here, John sees Jesus Christ step forward to begin His reign on earth.

****

❋ **ILLUSTRATION:** There is a chorus in Handel's *Messiah* that comes from this passage. It is one of the most beautiful, exquisite pieces of worship music that has ever been written. This is a perfect place to pause and listen to the words of this chorus:

> *"Hallelujah! for the Lord God Omnipotent reigneth.*
> *The Kingdom of this world is become the Kingdom of our Lord, and of His Christ:*
> *and He shall reign for ever and ever.*
> *King of kings, Lord of lords."*

****

Revelation 12–14
- From worship to war—war has been declared and three strong characters are introduced.
  - ~ **Satan:** He will bring his all into the battle. He is angry and his attacks against believers will increase greatly. He is referred to as the "red dragon."
  - ~ **The Antichrist:** He is "the beast." He will be a government or a political leader who will have incredible charisma and power—the people on earth will be drawn to him and will follow him.
  - ~ **The False Prophet:** He will point to the beast. He will encourage people to worship him.

- These three—the dragon, the beast, and the false prophet—make up the triune evil small "g" god. This satanic trinity is at work in the world.
  - ~ They will lie.
  - ~ They will deceive.
  - ~ They will destroy.

- God will now bring His last seven judgments. They are more intense than the others.

E. The seven BOWL judgments are poured out.

<u>Revelation 15–16</u>

1. Bowl One: Malignant SORES are upon those who worship the beast.

- Note the word "malignant." It means "grievous and distressing."
- These distressing sores come upon those who took the mark of the beast.

2. Bowl Two: The sea becomes BLOOD and everything in it dies.

3. Bowl Three: All RIVERS and springs become blood.

- At this point, many have been martyred.
- The evil triune wanted the blood of the martyrs:
  - ~ They took the blood of the prophets.
  - ~ They poured out the blood of Jesus Christ.
- With this judgment, it is as if God says, "You want blood? I am going to give you blood."
  - ~ All water sources turn to blood.
- All living creatures in the seas die—bringing a horrible stench of death.

4. Bowl Four: The sun SCORCHES men.

- The sun will heat up to the point of burning men's bodies, but not killing them—just great pain.

5. Bowl Five: All becomes DARK.

- People are in excruciating pain—they are crying out and chewing on their tongues.
- BUT—they will NOT bow their knee to God.

- They are in pain and in the dark—yet still shake their fists at God, blaspheming God Almighty.
- They blame God for their situation! They refuse to repent.

6. Bowl Six: The Euphrates DRIES up; nations gather for war.

- This is a necessary preparation for the war that is to take place.

7. Bowl Seven: It is DONE; the wrath of God is complete.

- There will be no more trumpets, no more seals, no more bowls.

REVELATION
Theme: God's Final Victory

✠ **Revelation 16:17** "Then the seventh angel poured out his bowl upon the air, and a loud voice came out of the temple from the throne, saying, 'It is done.'"

F. The second coming of Christ is described.

Revelation 19

- In his revelation, John shows us so much pain and suffering, but here all of heaven cries out:

1. Christ's coming is ANNOUNCED.

✠ **Revelation 19:1b** "Hallelujah! Salvation and glory and power belong to our God …"

- Christ, the warrior, is making Himself ready!

2. Christ comes with His ARMIES.

✠ **Revelation 19:11** "And I saw heaven opened, and behold, a white horse, and He who sat on it is called Faithful and True, and in righteousness He judges and wages war."

✠ **Revelation 19:13** "He is clothed with a robe dipped in blood, and His name is called The Word of God."

> ★ **TEACHING TIP:**
> *What a picture! For as far as one can see there is white with a crimson robe leading forth into battle!*

- His robe is dipped in blood—signifying the blood of those to be judged.
- We see a picture of judgment and victory.

✠ **Revelation 19:14** "And the armies which are in heaven, clothed in fine linen, white and clean, were following Him on white horses."

- The armies are saints—chosen, called, and faithful.

3. Christ is VICTORIOUS.

- John makes it clear that there is no need to worry—the battle belongs to the Lord and He will be victorious!

✠ **Revelation 19:19–21** "And I saw the beast and the kings of the earth and their armies assembled to make war against Him who sat on the horse and against His army. And the beast was seized, and with him the false prophet who performed the signs in his presence, by which he deceived those who had received the mark of the beast and those who worshiped his image; these two were thrown alive into the lake of fire which burns with brimstone. And the rest were killed with the sword which came from the mouth of Him who sat on the horse, and all the birds were filled with their flesh."

REVELATION
Theme: God's Final Victory

G. The millennial <u>KINGDOM</u> is established on earth for one thousand years.

Revelation 20

- It appears, at this point, that Christ will reign on earth for one thousand years and it is called the "millennium."
- During this time, there will be absolute peace.
- At the end of the millennium, it appears that Satan is released from the abyss.

- In Revelation 20:7–10, Satan returns—briefly.
  - ~ He is released from his prison.
  - ~ He will come once more to deceive the nations.
  - ~ He will once more wage war—it will be quick and decisive.
  - ~ Because Satan will once more be defeated—forever.
    - * He will spend eternity in the lake of fire and brimstone with the beast and false prophet.

H. The <u>NEW</u> Jerusalem is described as coming down from heaven, the eternal home for those who names are written in the Book of Life.

Revelation 21–22

- The new Jerusalem will come down out of heaven.
- It will be the home for believers for all eternity.
- There will be no suffering, no death.
- God Himself will bend down and wipe away every tear.
- There will be no need for a physical temple because Jesus Christ will reign supreme.
- Jesus Christ will be the light … the center … the all in all of the new Jerusalem!
- We, as believers, will live with Him in perfection and joy—with sinless bodies—forever and ever.

FINAL THOUGHTS AND APPLICATION

"Behold, I am coming quickly, and My reward is with Me,
to render to every man according to what he has done.
I am the Alpha and the Omega,
the first and the last, the beginning and the end."
                                        Revelation 22:12–13

REVELATION
Theme: God's Final Victory

"'I, Jesus, have sent My angel to testify to you these things for the churches.
I am the root and the descendant of David, the bright morning star.'
The Spirit and the bride say, 'Come.'
And let the one who hears say, 'Come.'
And let the one who is thirsty come;
let the one who wishes take the water of life without cost."
Revelation 22:16–17

"He who testifies to these things says, 'Yes, I am coming quickly.' Amen.
Come, Lord Jesus. The grace of the Lord Jesus be with all. Amen."
Revelation 22:20–21

❖ **FINAL APPLICATION:** **The King is coming! Therefore, worship with devotion, serve with passion, and live in the truth of His Word.**

OTHER LETTERS AND REVELATION AT A GLANCE

****

CHARTS

SET II

OTHER LETTERS AND REVELATION AT A GLANCE

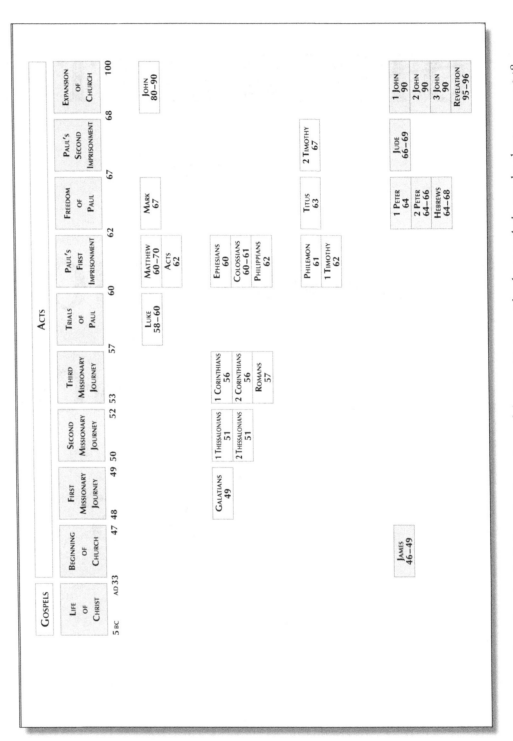

To see how these books fit into the chronology of the New Testament books as a whole, see the chart on page 248.

Hebrews

The Superiority Of:		
The **Person** of Christ over Prophets Angels Moses	The **Work** of Christ in Priesthood Covenant Sacrifices	The **Walk** of Christ-Followers in Faith Endurance Love
1:1 4:13	4:14 10:18	10:19 13:25

James

TESTS of Faith					
Trials and Temptations	Favoritism	The Tongue	Friendship with the World	Mistreatment	Suffering
TRAITS of Faith					
Hearer and Doer	Faith and Works	Wise Behavior	Humility	Endurance	Prayer
1	2	3	4	5:1-12	5:13-20

1 Peter

"This is the true grace of God."	"Stand firm in it!"	
SALVATION What Peter saw Jesus provide through His death on the cross	**SUBMISSION** What Peter struggled with in his relationship with Jesus	**SUFFERING** What Peter did not do well the night Jesus was arrested
1:1 2:10	2:11 2:12	3:13 5:14

2 Peter

CULTIVATION of Christian Character True Behavior 1	CONDEMNATION of False Teachers False Behavior and False Belief 2	COUNTERACTION to Mockers True Belief 3
Be on your guard so that you are not carried away by the error of unprincipled men. (2 Peter 3:17)		

2 Peter

1 Peter	2 Peter
Suffering from the Outside	Apostasy from the Inside
Remain Strong	Remain Faithful
Emphasis on Submission	Emphasis on Knowledge
Be Holy	Be Mature
Personal Attacks	Doctrinal Attacks
How to Respond to Enemies	How to Resist Error

1 John

Fellowship with God		
Walking in LIGHT Key Verses: 1:5-7	Walking in LOVE Key Verses: 4:7-8	Walking in LIFE Key Verses: 5:11-12
1 2	3 4	5

2 John

John **COMMENDS** the Recipients	John **COMMANDS** the Recipients	John **CAUTIONS** the Recipients
For Walking in the Truth	To Love One Another	Against False Teachers
Key Verse: 4	Key Verse: 5	Key Verse: 10
1 4	5 6	7 13

3 John

The Faithfulness of Gaius	The Pride of Diotrephes	The Good Reputation of Demetrius	The Desire of John
Shows Hospitality	Refuses Hospitality	Needs Hospitality	Commends Hospitality
1 8	9 11	12	13 15

3 John

1 John	2 John	3 John
Fellowship with God	Fellowship with False Teachers	Fellowship with the Brethren
Seek It	Avoid It	Practice It

JUDE

Warning About False Teachers	Description of False Teachers	Defense Against False Teachers	Victory over False Teachers
Purpose of Jude	Reminder of Jude	Instruction of Jude	Doxology of Jude
1 4	5 16	17 23	24 25
Danger for the Believers		Duty of the Believers	

REVELATION

"The Things Which You Have Seen"	"The Things Which Are"	"The Things Which Will Take Place After These Things"
(1:19)	(1:19)	(1:19)
A Picture of Christ	A Picture of the Churches	A Picture of the Consummation
His Glory	Their Challenges	Its Finality
"I fell at His feet like a dead man." (1:17)	"Hear what the Spirit says to the churches." (2:7)	"Amen. Come, Lord Jesus." (22:20)
1	2–3	4–22

REVELATION: DAY ONE—CHART A

New Testament Books

Chronological Relationship of the New Testament Books

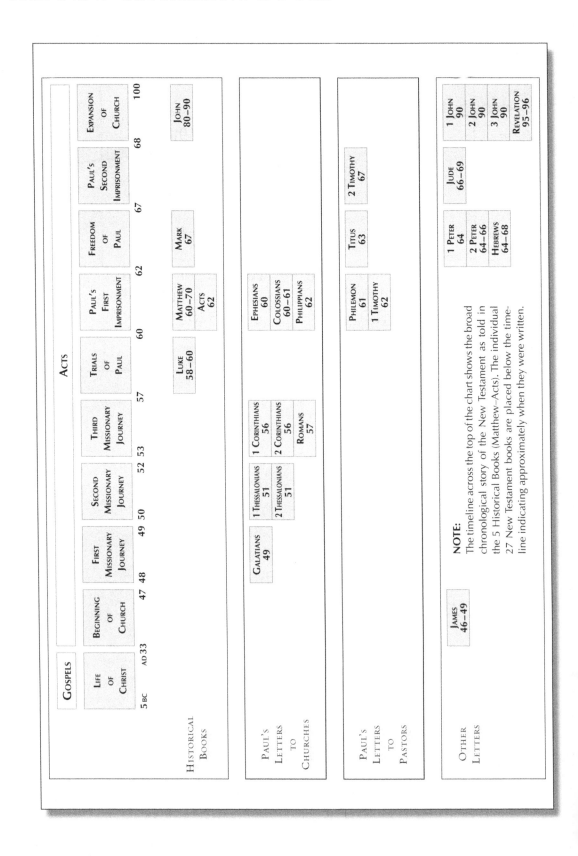

The chart contains the following information, organized by category:

GOSPELS / ACTS timeline (across the top):

5 BC — AD 33 — 47 48 49 50 52 53 57 60 62 67 68 100

- Life of Christ
- Beginning of Church
- First Missionary Journey
- Second Missionary Journey
- Third Missionary Journey
- Trials of Paul
- Paul's First Imprisonment
- Freedom of Paul
- Paul's Second Imprisonment
- Expansion of Church

Historical Books:
- Luke 58–60
- Matthew 60–70
- Acts 62
- Mark 67
- John 80–90

Paul's Letters to Churches:
- Galatians 49
- 1 Thessalonians 51
- 2 Thessalonians 51
- 1 Corinthians 56
- 2 Corinthians 56
- Romans 57
- Ephesians 60
- Colossians 60–61
- Philippians 62

Paul's Letters to Pastors:
- Philemon 61
- 1 Timothy 62
- Titus 63
- 2 Timothy 67

Other Letters:
- James 46–49
- 1 Peter 64
- 2 Peter 64–66
- Hebrews 64–68
- Jude 66–69
- 1 John 90
- 2 John 90
- 3 John 90
- Revelation 95–96

NOTE: The timeline across the top of the chart shows the broad chronological story of the New Testament as told in the 5 Historical Books (Matthew–Acts). The individual 27 New Testament books are placed below the timeline indicating approximately when they were written.

OTHER LETTERS

AND

REVELATION

AT A GLANCE

****

ADDITIONAL MAPS

MODERN STATES AND THE ANCIENT NEAR EAST

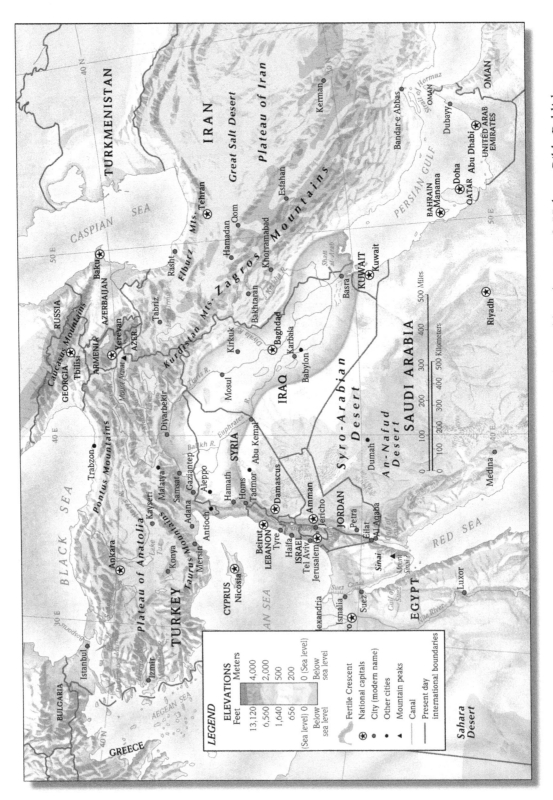

Modern States and the Ancient Near East from Holman Bible Atlas © 1998, Holman Bible Publishers. Used by permission.

THE EXPANSION OF CHRISTIANITY IN THE SECOND AND THIRD CENTURIES AD

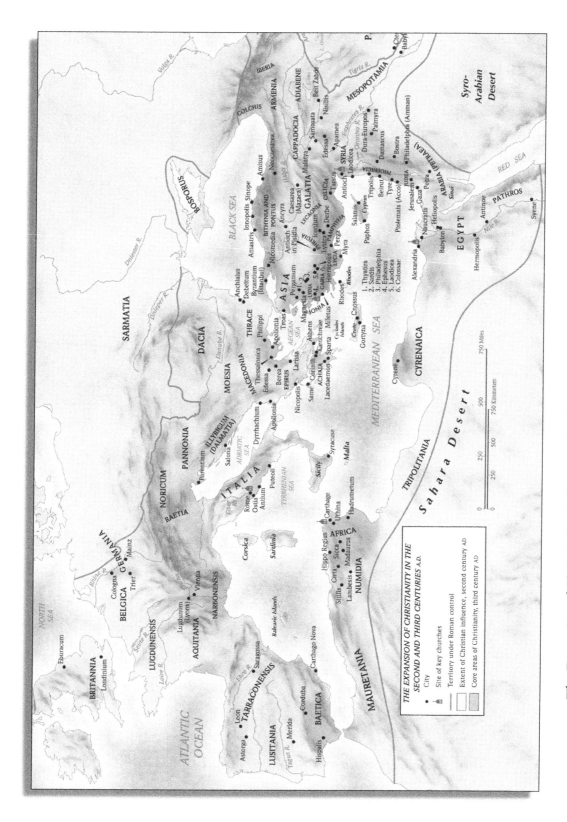

THE EXPANSION OF CHRISTIANITY IN THE SECOND AND THIRD CENTURIES A.D.

- • City
- ⛪ Site of key churches
- Territory under Roman control
- Extent of Christian influence, second century AD
- Core areas of Christianity, third century AD

The Expansion of Christianity in the Second and Third Centuries AD from Holman Bible Atlas
© 1998, Holman Bible Publishers. Used by permission.

Made in the USA
Coppell, TX
12 August 2023